Since completing Screen School and fil[ming] this book, I landed my first role on a pri[...] grateful to Screen School and The Ac[...] me fulfil my acting ambitions.
Joanna Barker

I got a place at drama school and couldn't have done it without Screen School.
Reece Soar

I uploaded my Screen School scenes to my Spotlight profile and managed to get an agent. I have since been auditioning regularly for film/TV/commercials.
Adriana Liu

Having my showreel scenes ready to share has opened up new windows of opportunity for me. They helped me score my first paid acting job. I'm on the ladder I've always wanted to be on, and now have productions in the calendar to look forward to.
Clare McGill

Two of the scenes featured in this book went straight into my showreel and I've since been signed up to an agent and been offered a number of paid casting opportunities.
Luke Willis

Most of the acting roles I've applied for on Mandy or Backstage always ask for a showreel. Now I have the showreel, the replies I am getting back when applying for roles are 70% higher than they were before.
Victoria Braithwaite

I would definitely recommend doing Screen School as you learn not just stuff about acting, but also about the industry and who you are as a person.
Hannah Sowter

It was such a confidence boost, it's engaging, exciting and super fun to take part in. I'd like to say Screen School is one of the best things to ever do in your life. I couldn't be happier with my scene and the people I worked with too.
Ryan McGovern

I can show evidence of my acting range thanks to the great teaching and production values at Screen School. It has truly been a blessing.
Andrew Henry

Tim, your knowledge is phenomenal. I'm so bloody glad I stumbled across your workshop and all you gorgeous people!
Kalisha Molloy

Have just watched the scenes and they are all amazing! Thanks again to all of you for making it one of the best weeks of my life!
Wahnetta Williamson

I've been involved in four Screen Schools now and they just get better and better! Whatever your acting dreams are...or your writing dreams...or just your dreams...it's life changing.
Denise Morton

It was an exceptional week! Tim you are bloody brilliant.
CC Anderson

This book and the scenes contained within are the copyright of The Actors Workshop Online / Screen School UK. The scene can be performed anywhere in the world free of charge, providing The Actors Workshop Online / Screen School are publicly credited.

This book may not be duplicated or reproduced. This book is not for re-sale. Any commercial use of this book and/or its contents is strictly prohibited without prior consent of The Actors Workshop Online / Screen School UK.

Copyright © The Actors Workshop / Screen School UK 2022

Published in the UK by The Actors Workshop

Cover by Tim Bryn Smith

ISBN 978-1-8384335-1-2

Contents

Foreword 1

Introduction 3

Friends and Enemies 9

False Pretences 9

Friends Reunited 12

The Wrong Track 16

Injustice 19

Cleansing Ritual 21

After the Vineyard 23

In Stitches 26

Rent Rise 28

Accountancy 32

Tell Her You Love Her 35

Dodgy Investments 37

Back to Skye 39

The Catch 41

Weddings and Parties 45

The Flirt 45

The Real Deal 48

Hayley 51

Wedding Bells 54

The Grandmother Standoff 58

Marrying the Wrong Kind 60

Dealer Dad 62

Dealer Dad Two 65

Not the Blue 68

The Grope 71

Bridal Jitters 75

Baby Talk 77

Studio Space 79

Hens 81

Too Posh to Imprison 83

Tent Peg 85

Her Song 88

Tarot 90

Funerals 93

The Dead Good Brothers 93

Nuts about You 97

Dad 100

Friendly Blackmail 102

Tough Crowd 105

The Lunchtime Mix-Up 107

Family Affairs 110

Worst Day Ever 113

Killed by Bears 116

Not a Fucking Charity 118

Seize the Day 121

Prison 123

Bending the Rules 123

The Plea 127

Sisterly and Brotherly Love 129

Prison Payback 132

The Suspect 134

I Have Rights 136

Stitched Up 138

For Callum 140

Too Late Now 142

Do-Gooder 144

Mother's Boy 146

Standing up for my Kids 148

Therapy 150

In the Workplace 150

Therapeutic Truth 153

Risking it All 156

Taking the Piss 159

Trigger 163

The Workplace Bully 167

Only Joking 169

Good Grief 171

Anger Management 173

Spinning Plates 176

The Affair 179

Doing my Bit 181

Work 183

Binary Code 183

Bitch Boss 185

Just the Job 187

Desperate Measures 190

Under Threat of Pineapple 192

Sister's Blessing 195

Driving School Dream 197

Midlife Crunch 200

Double Agent 202

Curriculum Vitae 204

On the Run 206

Waking the Lion 208

Serious Complaints 211

Coat Rage 213

Maternity Leave 215

Hope, Crushed 217

A Ratings Winner 219

Family and Relationships 221

Scuppered 221

Leaving 224

Right to Choose 226

Mature Attraction 228

Starting Again 230

Ultimatum 232

Hope 235

Name Your Price 237

The Ex 239

Priorities 243

Man to Man 245

Last Will and Testament 247

A Proposal 249

Wait for Me 251

Moral Relativity 253

I Love the Flow 255

Running Around 258

Activism 260

Acknowledgements 262

About Screen School 263

About the Actors Workshop 264

Foreword

Collaborating with someone who shares your enthusiasm and desire to push creative limits turns the workplace into an exciting land of innovative opportunity. Tim and I met on the Notts TV set for the programme *Sketch Up,* and we've worked closely together ever since, on a career trajectory that has opened a myriad of film industry doors for us.

Three years ago, Tim asked me to begin writing scenes for his brand-new Screen School course. This course – which runs several times a year – gives us the chance to create original scripts which offer the performers in each scene the chance to play nuanced, richly layered characters in a compelling situation. We then get the opportunity to tweak the lines in a live setting to ensure the dialogue packs the most powerful punch possible. All of the scenes in this book were written for Screen School. They are the end results of an intensely creative and collaborative process.

Writing for Screen School is always thought-provoking, and endless fun. Tim and I begin to prepare for each course by bouncing ideas off one another, looking for the best avenues to explore. I write each scene with a specific actor in mind, but the creative process doesn't end there. Over several days, the dialogue is developed both on camera and off, with Tim directing to ensure that each showreel has a memorable impact on the viewer. It's through the push-pull nature of this development process that we end up with the best scenes possible. What we have discovered is that, in just a few lines, it is possible to take the viewer on a micro-journey that leaves them desperate to find out more about a character, as well as the actor behind it.

As an award-winning screenwriter, I've worked with hundreds of different actors in film studios around the world, but still nothing can prepare you for that Screen School moment when a scene comes together perfectly. There's magic in the room as you watch it on the monitor, and a shiver runs down everyone's spine. This is rarely down to performance alone, but rather a combination of acting, direction and photography. We offer you these scenes in the hope that you'll create your own memorable showreels.

Sara Bodinar
Screen School writer-in-residence

Introduction

To get noticed as an actor, you need a showreel that gets attention from industry decision-makers. As an actor, teacher, director and producer, I can say without doubt that showreels are really important. Over the past twenty years I've studied countless reels and, through the Actors Workshop and Screen School, I've helped hundreds of actors to create stunning showreel material. I'm passionate about supporting actors to showcase their talent and pursue their dreams, and I'm incredibly lucky to be in a position to do so.

A showreel is a short, edited video, no more than a few minutes long, containing selected highlights of an actor's best screen work. Filmed footage from theatre plays or live stage productions will not convince industry gatekeepers that an actor deserves a role in a TV show or a movie. Showreels should only feature screen work.

One of the most badly kept secrets in the entertainment industry is that casting directors and producers rarely watch a whole showreel. In fact, they're likely to form an opinion of an actor's ability after the first ten seconds. Only if an actor has managed to keep their attention will the casting director be likely to skim through the rest of the reel, stopping at particularly stand-out visual moments. For this reason, actors should always place their best work first.

When casting directors are watching your reels, they'll focus on specific things. Do you fit the part? Are you natural and believable? Are you emotionally connected? What surprises are in your performance, and what unique qualities do you possess?

When I began my own career, over thirty-five years ago, one hundred percent of the castings I attended took place in person. These days, actors rarely get the chance to make a strong first impression in person in front of a casting panel. Now, most first-round auditions are held by self-tape and supported by a review of an actor's showreel. Given this, it's essential that your reel stands out. It's not unusual for actors to be cast on the strength of their showreels alone.

You should continually replace sections of your showreel with more recent work. Many fledgling actors have no choice but to try to assemble showreels from student or short film appearances, promos, commercials, and other low budget bits-and-bobs they work on. This kind of work can be a great learning curve but relying on inexperienced film-makers to provide you with polished cinematic footage can often be futile. Many an actor has wasted valuable time waiting for finished material to add to their showreels, only to discover it hasn't been filmed and edited to a professional standard. Common problems include poor sound quality and overexposed lighting. My point here is not to criticise amateurish footage, as we all need to start somewhere, but rather to encourage you not to be too reliant on visuals from amateur productions you've acted in. The longer you wait for your reel material, the more parts you might have missed out on.

Early on in your career, when you don't have the luxury of a wide selection of filmed material at your disposal, creating your own reel footage can be the most efficient way to get a foothold in the industry. Plus, with so many fantastic free online camera and editing courses available, picking up the basic skills to shoot your own scenes is often a preferred option. Mobile phone camera technology is so spectacular, there's really nothing stopping actors becoming controllers of their own destinies. It's often just about finding the right script material, which is where we hope this book will come in useful.

There is no exact science to the number of clips necessary to create a reel. If you have hours of incredible scene footage, it can be hard to decide what to include, but you must keep the total length down to a couple of minutes maximum. If you include multiple clips, keep them concise and focused on you and your character.

If you are an actor starting out, you probably don't yet have access to a wide selection of suitable material. In this case, a single scene can showcase you and be used as your showreel, until you gather more footage.

When writing showreel scripts, Sara and I strive to give actors the opportunity to showcase a wide emotional range, thus providing them with a great calling card in a stand-alone scene. Screen School alumni regularly use these scenes to win roles and land agents.

The scenes we write and produce have been so successful for our students that they return to Screen School again and again. Repeat attendees are able to accumulate a collection of high-quality filmed scenes and compile a varied, dynamic showreel. When edited together, the scenes in this book provide an impactful compilation of work that highlights a performer's true skillset.

YouTube is now clamping down harder than ever on actors extracting scene material from copyrighted films, TV shows and theatre plays to use in their showreels. In fact, we were recently told by a large publisher to remove a video from our own YouTube channel. The video in question featured one of our actors performing a two-minute monologue, extracted from a play.

By using scenes from this book in your showreel, you will not fall foul of any copyright laws, as you have our express permission to use them. All we ask is that you duly credit the authors. We also invite you to share your work with us, because we would love to see it.

As you will see from the following scenes, it's possible to take the viewer on a micro-journey that leaves them desperate to find out more about the character, and the actor behind it. This book contains a huge selection of scenes, well suited for a wide range of ages and genders. If there's a script you like, but it's the wrong age or gender for you, feel free to adapt the text to suit your needs and switch things up. Have fun, experiment, change the words to fit you like a glove, and make each scene your own.

Take time to find scenes that suit your type. Allow ample rehearsal time not only to block and rehearse the scenes, but also to develop the character's back story. Give them a full emotional life and explore their relationships with the other characters, both on and off screen. Good acting is specific acting. Be sure to leave no stone unturned in creating a fully rounded character.

Look for opportunities to explore emotional contrast in your performance. For example, think about how you might perform 'sad' scenes in such a way that allows you to avoid presenting them in a predictably 'sad' way. Emotional complexity is far more compelling when characters try to hold back their emotions. This tactic will cause the audience to connect with the story you're telling in a deeper way, create more intrigue, and make you more memorable as a performer. The most exciting moment in a performance is when a character can no longer hold back the tidal wave of emotions they have been building up, and it all comes rushing out.

In this book we have grouped together the scenes according to their themes and settings. The scenes are especially accessible as the majority require little in the way of specialist sets, locations, props, make up, or other elaborate production/post-production elements. This means you should be able to film most of these scenes using simple, inexpensive locations and easily sourced costumes. Of course, feel free to adapt any of the scenes to suit your production needs and budget.

To help with your selection process, we have included QR codes next to some of the scenes featured in this book. By scanning the code on your smart device, you will be taken to a YouTube video of the original scene, performed by Screen School alumni. We hope these examples will both inform and inspire you. We highly recommend that you don't just try to copy the performances you see. In the same way you would be unlikely to recreate an exact replica of Robert De Niro's *Taxi Driver* speech for your showreel, you should concentrate on making a scene your own. Adding your own creativity to the scenes in this book will ensure you play to your individual strengths.

Tim Bryn Smith
Founder & Director, The Actors Workshop Online

Friends and Enemies

False Pretences

A rich man welcomes in Betty, a homeless woman, under false pretences. She shuffles in, looking at him suspiciously. He opens the fridge.

BETTY

Got a great place here.

MAN

Make yourself at home. Do you like lasagne?

BETTY

Yeah…yeah, I do.

MAN

Spare room's through there (*loosens his tie*) and you look like you could use a shower (*takes tie off*).

BETTY

A warm shower would be amazing.

MAN

Mind if I join you? (*starts rolling up his sleeves*)

BETTY

What?

MAN

Well, you're getting a meal, and a bed.

BETTY

Are you being serious right now?

You are.

I told you why I was on the streets. I told you that I'm not a prostitute. I'm on the streets because I wouldn't fuck my stepdad. You know that! And yet you think that I want to fuck you? I'm out.

Betty walks off, the man follows. Betty grabs the knife and turns on him.

BETTY

Get back! You lied to me. You fucking lied to me! Don't think I won't hurt you cos I fucking will. I've heard about fucking guys like you…you piece of shit. Give me the fucking keys. I said give me the fucking keys!

MAN

It's not locked.

BETTY

Don't move. Fucking stay right there.

Betty moves to the door keeping her eyes on the man.

You fucking prick!

Betty leaves flat.

Friends Reunited

Tough but loyal Jade has just been released from prison. She turns up to her friend's house thinking she'll be able to stay for a few days, but her friend turns her away.

JADE

Oh my god this place is amazing! Man, I am so glad to be out. Yeah, I've been waiting to hear if I got parole all week, and then yesterday they were like yeah you can go. And I was like really? Aaaand you know here I am, but I am so fucking relieved.

FRIEND

I bet you are…so do you want a little drink-y drink?

JADE

Yeah…have you got Capri Sun?

FRIEND

Capri Sun?

JADE

Yeah.

FRIEND

Okay...whatever.

With a surprised look the friend reaches into the fridge and pulls out a Capri-Sun which she hands to Jade.

FRIEND

Here you go.

JADE

Thanks babe. Mmmm, this is peng! Thanks for letting me stay by the way.

FRIEND

Ahh. Yeah uhm, yeah you can't stay here!

JADE

What?

FRIEND

You can't stay here.

JADE

Jacks... I've got nowhere else to go.

FRIEND

This isn't my place...and you know how Joel gets.

JADE

Legit...it's just going to be a few nights, just until social services can get me a bedsit. Legit I'm going to be on the streets! You know that Jake was going to kill me if he finds I've come back. C..can't you just talk to him?

FRIEND

No, I can't.

JADE

I've just fucking done time for you! Three fucking months!

FRIEND

What?

JADE

This is the thanks I get?! You ungrateful little shit!

Friend laughs.

JADE

You know what? I'm fucking staying. I'm fucking staying here. I'm fucking staying. You're going to talk to him otherwise…I'm going to tell him that you used to suck dick for money.

FRIEND

Fine. I'll talk to him.

JADE

S'what I thought.

Friend leaves, Jade continues drinking Capri Sun.

JADE

So fucking good.

The Wrong Track

Gemma fell asleep on the train. Now she's miles from home late at night. She has gone back to the house of an old friend who was sitting next to her on the train.

GEMMA

I am so sorry about this. It must be a massive inconvenience. I'll be gone first thing in the morning, I promise. I've checked and there's a train at nine am.

FRIEND

Don't worry about it. I know it's been ages since we last saw each other!

GEMMA

I know! I can't believe I missed the station, it's so kind of you to put me up.

FRIEND

It's no problem! Would you like a glass of wine?

GEMMA

I've had enough thanks.

FRIEND

Oh, come on! You used to drink more than us back in the day.

GEMMA

No…

FRIEND

Well, at least can I take your coat?

GEMMA

Oh! Yeah.

Gemma takes off her coat and gives it to him. He just chucks it onto the seat Gemma was in and looks at her.

FRIEND

You look good. Haven't changed. Still the same nice figure…Shame to even hide it.

GEMMA

Maybe this is a bad idea. I'm putting you out.

FRIEND

You're really not. You knew what you were doing when you accepted my offer of a bed.

GEMMA

You've got the wrong idea. That's not what I meant at all.

You need to move. Move!

Friend moves aside and Gemma leaves.

Injustice

Jean is being consoled by a friend after the acquittal of the man who was charged with raping her.

JEAN

He denied everything.

FRIEND

You're joking?

JEAN

No. It all came down to one message I sent him on WhatsApp after he'd... Sexually provocative. That's what they called it. It said, 'Yeah I'd love to do it in a jacuzzi'. I mean, am I mad cos anyone with half a brain would know why I sent that message.

FRIEND

Yeah, cos you were bloody scared?

JEAN

He knew where I lived. I was on my own. He's only a street away. And I just thought…I just thought…I just thought that if he had to ask the neighbour about the jacuzzi, that would give me an extra ten minutes to get to my sister's. You know in case he came after me. But according to his legal team, I'm the sexually provocative one.

FRIEND

I can't believe you've been through all this. Is this the first time you've told anyone?

JEAN

Yeah.

FRIEND

God, you've been so strong… been so brave. Listen, you're going to get through this. You are going to get through this, okay? Come on, I'm here for you. You're going to get through it. You're going to be alright. You're going to be good. Okay?

Cleansing Ritual

Toby is doing a cleansing ritual he saw on YouTube to help his best friend get over her ex.

TOBY

Give me your hand.

They join hands.

We dip it in the cedar oil and then lean forward until our noses are touching the sage. Repeat after me. Begone from this house, lingering twattiness of Neil. Oh he of too much fake tan and…

Toby breaks off and looks at his friend.

What were you actually thinking? He was a minger!

BEST FRIEND

Get on with it. How do you know how to do this anyway?

TOBY

YouTube. Trust me, after this cleansing ceremony, you won't ever think of that bastard again.

BEST FRIEND

Good!

TOBY

Be gone from this house…

The ex walks in and sits on the table, upsetting the sage display.

EX

What the bloody hell's this then? You making a salad, Toby?

TOBY

Don't look into his eyes, Nic. His power is diminishing.

EX

(To Nic) Do you wanna get a Nando's?

BEST FRIEND

Yeah, alright then.

TOBY

Oh, for fucks sake.

The best friend gets up to leave. Toby glares at them, waits for them to leave, then kicks the table.

(Shouts towards the door) Guess I'll be watching *The Crown* on my own then!

After the Vineyard

Bitchy Louise got crazy drunk and can't remember the night before. Embarrassed, she asks the rando on the sofa next to her what happened.

LOUISE

Hi, I'm Louise. I can't remember anything. Did we…?

SOFA RANDO

No. I wanted to, but you told me you were too drunk to make a sensible decision.

LOUISE

Wow! Okay good. So how did we meet? I guess, what I'm trying to say is…where am I?

SOFA RANDO

We met upstairs. This is Luke's house. It was Luke's party.

LOUISE

Who's Luke?

SOFA RANDO

Luke from the Vineyard!

LOUISE

Am I on a vineyard? Which country am I in?

SOFA RANDO

No! Not vineyard as in wine… as in…you know, the church on Castle Boulevard.

LOUISE

Right.

SOFA RANDO

You and your friends went to the service and then afterwards Luke invited you to come here. That's what you told me. You were a bit tired, I think. It was a bit hard to make out what you were saying.

LOUISE

So I didn't do anything weird?

SOFA RANDO

Oh no. We had a quick dance and then came down here.

LOUISE

Okay great

At that moment Louise's friend comes into the room, holding Louise's dress.

FRIEND

There you are! Oh my god, you were so wasted last night.

LOUISE

Yeah, but it sounds like I was quite sensible!

FRIEND

Who told you that?! You took all your clothes off for a start. We covered you up with a blanket, but you kept telling us how horny you felt, then you ran around flashing everyone….

LOUISE

Oh noooo! Don't tell me anymore!

In Stitches

Lynette is new to the area and has joined a knitting stitch to make new friends.

LYNETTE

(*To the woman next to her*) I'm a bit rusty. My life's still in boxes all over the new flat. I couldn't find my own needles, so I got these at the charity shop.

Lynette holds up her needles.

Which way up do I hold them?

The woman next to her take the needles out of Lynette's hands and turns them the other way up.

LYNETTE

Can I get a wee bit of your wool...?

WOMAN

Mm...I kind of need it. Didn't you bring any?

LYNETTE

It's a fair cop. I can't knit. I just came here to meet new people. Are you going to kick me out?

The woman laughs.

WOMAN

No.

LYNETTE

Thanks! To be completely honest, I'm not creative at all. I couldn't even draw you a picture of a scarf, let alone bloody make one! I've started a new job at the university. So I can tell you all about polymers and compounds...but stitches...not a thing! I'm willing to learn though... So, what do I do with these again?

Lynette brandishes her needles.

Rent Rise

Fun-loving, volatile actor Florence's landlord is coming round. She thinks he's bringing her a package that was delivered in error. She is rehearsing lines while chopping vegetables.

FLORENCE

It wasn't about the money. I didn't need the money. No…shit. Okay. It wasn't about the money. I didn't need the money. It wasn't about the money. I didn't need the money.

LANDLORD

Hello!

FLORENCE

Oh, hey mate! I massively appreciate it. Can you leave the parcel on the side?

LANDLORD

There is no parcel.

FLORENCE

What do you mean? You literally just texted me saying you were picking up the parcel from Lucy's?

LANDLORD

I've brought you something very special instead.

FLORENCE

Ooh, what is it?

Landlord pulls an envelope out of his jacket.

What is it? An invite?

Florence opens the envelope, her excitement fades.

Is this like, some sort of joke?

LANDLORD

That is a Section 13 rent notice.

FLORENCE

Seriously? Like you're actually expecting me to pay £500 a month more?

LANDLORD

Well, it's a very lovely flat, isn't it?

FLORENCE

Yes, it is very nice and I can't afford that, so you can take that back thank you.

Florence hands back the envelope and turns back to her kitchen table to continue chopping vegetables.

LANDLORD

Florence, if you're struggling to pay we can always enter negotiations.

FLORENCE

What exactly do you mean by negotiations?

LANDLORD

Well, you know your lovely friend Lucy in the upstairs penthouse? How do you think she affords the rent?

FLORENCE

I don't know. I think you should probably leave now.

LANDLORD

I've seen the look on your face. You love it. Don't you? You love it.

FLORENCE

Don't you fucking dare do this again.

Florence threatens him with the knife.

Don't you fucking dare.

LANDLORD

Come on.

FLORENCE

Get out! Get out! Leave! Or I'll call the police.

LANDLORD

Very well…I wish you all the best with that endeavour.

Toodaloo.

The landlord leaves.

FLORENCE

Fuck…oh my god.

Accountancy

Krane and The Accountant are tied up, huddled in a dark corner of the warehouse.

KRANE

They're going to kill us. You realise that don't you?

THE ACCOUNTANT

What was I supposed to do? Let those bastards loose on two innocent kids?

KRANE

This is not my fucking problem. I had nothing to do with this shit.

THE ACCOUNTANT

They told us. If we told them the codes, they'd let the kids go.

KRANE

We can't help anyone if we are dead, can we? What use are we if we are dead, Tom?

THE ACCOUNTANT

You got me involved in this shit in the first place. I'm just a fucking accountant.

KRANE

And I'm not exactly Pablo Escobar, am I?

There is shouting outside. They sit. Listening.

And where are Sam and Amelia now? Did they let them go?

THE ACCOUNTANT

I think so.

KRANE

What do you mean, 'you think so'?! You mean you don't even know?

THE ACCOUNTANT

Yes! Yes, they are safe! They're safe.

KRANE

You put their lives before ours. I don't give a shit if they're 'just kids' Tom. You had no right. You had no right to do that. I want my own kids someday. I don't want to fucking die. And I am not going to fucking die. Do you understand me? I am not going to fucking die.

Two armed guards enter.

GUARD 1

You. Get up. Now.

Neither of them moves. The guard grabs Krane and drags him away kicking and screaming.

KRANE

Get the fuck off me. Take him. He's the one you want. This is his fault. It's his fault!

Tom sits. Waits. The sound of gun fire outside.

Tell Her You Love Her

Naomi has been kidnapped. She is lying down in the corner of the warehouse. She has been badly injured and is being looked after by another hostage, Lee. Lee gives her a drink. He's trying to care for her.

NAOMI

You remind me of my nephew in America. He's a doctor.

LEE

Dunno about that. He must be well clever.

Naomi starts slipping in and out of consciousness.

Hey! Hey! Can you hear me? I need you to wake up. What's your name?

He spots Naomi's medical bracelet.

Naomi? No way. That's my mum's name. Can you believe that? That's mad... Before this, the last thing I said to her... I called her a stuck-up bitch. I wish I could take it back.

Naomi looks at Lee, her eyes widen. Naomi's hand reaches for Lee's.

NAOMI

Tell her you love her. When you see her.

LEE

I will. I will. I promise.

She starts to fade away just as a captor walks in.

CAPTOR

Quiet!

Naomi whimpers.

I said shut it!

LEE

She needs a doctor. You need to get a doctor in here quick!

The captor drags Lee off at gunpoint.

She needs help please! No! Please!

Naomi protests but is too weak to move.

NAOMI

Please. No.

Dodgy Investments

Helen is the wife of a Russian billionaire. She has been abducted along with the cartel's lawyer, Julia. They are being held in an abandoned warehouse.

HELEN

You told me it was a portfolio investment. Not an arms deal. How could you keep this from me?

JULIA

I couldn't have stopped this.

HELEN

You lied to me. For ten years. After everything I did for you. Your family.

JULIA

If he pays the ransom, we'll get out of here.

HELEN

I don't care anymore. I've lost everything. It's all gone.

JULIA

We need to stick together. Do you understand?

Two armed guards come in.

GUARD 1

He's paid half, one of you gets to leave.

HELEN

I've got £4 million in a safety deposit box. It's yours. All of it.

The guard motions for Helen to get up.

JULIA

What? Where are you going? No, please! I can help you; I can get you money!

Helen walks away as the guard raises the gun towards Julia. He pulls the trigger.

Back to Skye

After having been kidnapped, shot and left for dead, Sean and Jess are tied up in a dilapidated warehouse. They talk in hushed tones.

JESS

Hey! You promised me mojitos in the Maldives this summer. Did you forget that? You promised me.

SEAN

You know I don't like planes, babe.

JESS

Just so you know, we are never going back to Blackpool. Don't even think about it.

Sean manages a weak smile.

Skye. You can take me back to Skye, though. Coral Beach.

They share a knowing look. Sean's eyes begin to twinkle. Jess laughs, so does Sean but his laugh turns to coughing. He settles.

SEAN

I love you.

His pain increases. He closes his eyes tightly. Then he begins to fade.

JESS

I love you too.

He's back, momentarily.

SEAN

I need you to... tell Angel. How proud I am. Tell her how much...

JESS

No. You have to get us out of here. Please...

Sean digs deep to find the strength. There's a glimmer. They're interrupted by an armed guard who arrives and drags Jess away. She screams. Sean urges himself half up, he is powerless. Jess is brought before him pleading.

Please no, no! God no, please!

A gun shot.

SEAN

No!

The Catch

Two friends share are having drinks in the pub.

SAM

Cheers!

CLARE

Cheers!

SAM

It's so nice to do this again.

CLARE

I know. I don't think we've done this since you moved to Ravenshead.

SAM

Has it been that long?

CLARE

At least, yeah!

SAM

You were seeing that guy with the Disney tattoos.

CLARE

Jesus. What a ride that was.

They laugh and drink.

So come on, fill me in. Who are you seeing at the moment?

SAM

Oh, I've been really busy with work.

CLARE

Sam. What are you hiding from me?

SAM

Nothing!

CLARE

Sammy Sam! I know you!

SAM

Ok. Ok…so I might have seen Douglas recently.

CLARE

Oh my god! Doug! Oh my god. No. Doug?

SAM

It's not like it's a big deal!

CLARE

Were you with him last night? You were, weren't you!

SAM

Yeah, but it was fine.

CLARE

Did he stay over?

SAM

Maybe.

CLARE

Eww. Did he do that thing again?

SAM

What thing?

CLARE

You know what I'm talking about.

SAM

I'm not sure I...

CLARE

Sam! You told me he likes to watch you sleep...and then...

She makes an awkward sexual gesture with her hand.

SAM

Clare! Don't do that!

CLARE

It's so weird, Sam. Aren't you freaked out by it?

SAM

I'm not sure it's that weird.

CLARE

Trust me, it is weird! I ask all the guys I sleep with if it's weird and they all say it's fucking weird. And, you know, I've slept with a lot of guys.

SAM

He always clears it up afterwards!

CLARE

That does not mean he's a great catch Sam.

SAM

He bought me a really nice candle.

CLARE

You're properly clutching at straws now.

SAM

It was an expensive one.

CLARE

No Sammy. Just no!

Weddings and Parties

The Flirt

Sociable, flirty and manipulative Rupert is hosting a party. He decides to play a little game with his guests.

RUPERT

Dear…would you mind getting me a splash more?

PARTNER

Seeing as it's your birthday.

Partner leaves to refill Rupert's drink.

SEXY WOMAN

It's stunning.

RUPERT

The place isn't too shabby. It's enough for me…and her.

SEXY WOMAN

And you have a snooker table?

RUPERT

You noticed.

SEXY WOMAN

You must play me tonight... meow.

RUPERT

Time for a game...ding ding ding ding ding ding...

Crowd cheer.

RUPERT

Ladies and gentlemen...everyone, put your keys in here. You know where this is going.

As he speaks, Rupert finds a bowl and then starts holding it out to the crowd. People start putting their car keys in the bowl.

Jean, I like it.... Two keys? No no... and I'm sure you won't protest when the host decides to go first.

There are general cries of uh-oh / YES! Woah.

Rupert makes very obvious eye contact with the sexy woman.

Without dropping eye contact, Rupert fishes out a key (with a distinctive keyring – so he can feel it) and waves it at the person he's looking at.

RUPERT

Oh, that's a surprise.

SEXY WOMAN

They're not my keys.

RUPERT

What?

MAN

They're mine.

RUPERT

I had you all going, didn't I?

MAN

Hold on!

The man grabs Rupert and makes a suggestive move on him.

Rupert is taken away by the man to the cheers of the crowd.

The Real Deal

An engagement party is in full swing. Adi clinks a glass and the revellers cheer, excited for his speech.

ADI

Right, settle down everyone. Thanks again for coming tonight. As you all know, we are gathered here tonight to celebrate the engagement of my near and dear friend Phil. But what can I say about Phil that we don't already know? Back at school, me, him and another guy used to be known as the three musketeers, and we used to get into all sorts of scrapes. I mean, I remember the time you hit Miss Edwards in the face with a bag of books and…

PHIL

Adi, we didn't go to the same school…we went to youth orchestra together.

ADI

Youth orchestra! Right, that's where we met. I played the clarinet, as you all know and you the flugelhorn… he was a very good player. Like that y'know.

Adi mimes playing the instrument.

PHIL

Guitar. I played the guitar.

ADI

I'm just messing with you man, calm down. You've been such a great friend to me for all these years, and I've been nothing but horrible to him. I mean, I'm self-absorbed, forgetful. I remember that one time I missed his twenty-first because I was on a date! And she wasn't even that good looking! But uhm, it wasn't until that time I was at the hospital when I realised how good a friend you really were, because no one else here would've spent hours by my bedside playing chess and uhm, talking about books and films and music and all that. I honestly could've died were it not for you.

Phil addresses the room.

PHIL

I wasn't doing anything else. I'd already finished *Game of Thrones* so…that wasn't the first near death experience you've had…

ADI

No, it wasn't…to put it lightly, ladies and gentlemen, I would not be standing here today were it not for Phil…so, yeah thanks.

PHIL

You're welcome.

ADI

You've been such a great friend to me all these years. This fellow - he's the real deal, everyone, and I want you to know. I'm going to make it up to you. So, you, me, and the rest of the guys here. Vegas. Tonight. All paid for by me.

Crowd Cheers.

ADI

Phil and Shannon everyone… I love you, man.

PHIL

Love you too.

Hayley

Lee is at an engagement party boasting about how he once spent a night with the bride to be.

LEE

Me and her (*nods his head towards the bride to be*) had a very interesting night in a Wolverhampton hotel once! She loved it! She was all over me! Pure filth! Let's just say if she's planning on wearing white on her wedding day, I can testify to Tez not being her first.

FRIEND

Tez's ears must be burning. He's coming over! Does he even know?

LEE

Nooo! Don't you say anything either.

Tez arrives and grins at them both.

FRIEND

Alright Tez?

TEZ

Alright lads, you having a nice time?

FRIEND

Great night, thanks. Congratulations.

TEZ

Thank you.

FRIEND

Lee here was just telling me about how he knows Hayley from way back in the day.

TEZ

Oh yeah?

LEE

Well yeah, yeah, I mean I sort of did.

TEZ

I thought you only met her for the first time two weeks ago?

LEE

I must've got it wrong. Different girl it was. I can see that now. My mistake. Tez…great party, yeah anyway I've got to get off early…cos you know…

Lee starts walking away.

See you…

Glasses are rubbish now…going to have to get some new ones.

TEZ

What the fuck was all that about?

FRIEND

Uhm, just said he knows Hayley from way back in the day.

TEZ

Fucking arsehole.

Wedding Bells

Drunken, grudge-holding Spencer is at an engagement party, clinking his glass, about to give a speech nobody has asked for.

SPENCER

Okay everyone. I've got something I want to say. Uh, you can save your boos for the church ceremony! You know that part where the vicar says if anyone has any objections… not because I have any objections personally. No, I've nothing against Sol and his sexy bride, Henrietta. You look stunning tonight by the way darling, but I prefer the yellow one-piece you wore on a beach in St Tropez on holiday with your mum…that's a Facebook go-to for me if you know what I mean…

Some of the crowd laughs, a few people look outraged.

HENRIETTA *to* **SOL**

Are you going to say something?

SOL

Steady on mate.

SPENCER

Where was I? Booing in the church, that's it. I want you to join me. Seeing as we're all here together…it's time we denounced a history of ecclesiastical torture! Sol and I were scholarship boarders at the John the Baptist College for Young Gentlemen for five very long years, as most of you will know. And we were subjected to the most horrific sadism that resulted in years of therapy.

SOL

Where's this going Spencer?

SPENCER

We were subjected to years of (*mumbles*)… I'm getting mixed up…and during that time we were subjected to the most horrific sadism that resulted in years of therapy and my inability to form any sort of meaningful relationship…with anyone. Sol has been there for me through all of it. But I can't stand by and allow this shocking endorsement of the institution that ruined my life (*crying*). Sorry, Henrietta love. I know you think you're religious, but I suspect a large part of your venue decision might have been how lovely the eaves would look in the photos…

SOL

Spencer. Don't do this.

SPENCER

Don't speak out?

SOL

Not now.

SPENCER

Is it not ideal timing? It's their fucking church, Sol.

SOL

Stop it!

SPENCER

If not at this golden opportunity, then when?

SOL

Well, if you can't stop yourself…

SPENCER

I don't think I can stop myself.

SOL

Then don't bother coming to the wedding at all.

SPENCER

Really? You're saying don't come. You're picking them?

SOL

I'm picking my wife!

SPENCER

Fuck your wife!

SOL

Right. You've crossed a line there!

SPENCER

Uhm…I'm sorry…I didn't mean that.

SOL

Sorry everyone, I just think he's had a bit too much to drink.

HENRIETTA

Don't.

SPENCER

Uhm, to the happy couple!

CROWD (*lacklustre*)

To…the happy…couple

SPENCER

I'm going to go.

Spencer walks off, hurt by Sol.

The Grandmother Standoff

Witchy mother of the bride, Carmen, can't stop herself rising to the bait of her daughter's soon to be mother-in-law

CARMEN

I don't see what's wrong in mentioning kids! It's not as if they're spring chickens, is it? They need to get on it. I mean obviously hang on for a week, until after the final dress fitting...and the big day, but after that...what's the point in wasting time? I'll be a brilliant grandmother...as will you too, I'm sure, in your own way, but I'm going to be the one who keeps them grounded in this crazy world. You can put too much emphasis on not eating the wrong things...they need to experience life. Life! Free from society's constraints, free to move between borders, just free.

MOTHER-IN-LAW

Just like you, you mean? No job, no house, no real teeth...?

CARMEN

Do you know the price for offending someone like me? I'll show you. *Has ki cafa*! (*made up language*)

MOTHER-IN-LAW

What the hell was that? Have you just put a curse on me??

CARMEN

I warned her you know. Jacob won't understand our ways. And his mother's got a stick up her arse so long it's stopped her brain working, but she wouldn't listen to me. This marriage is happening and I'm watching out for my daughter. Always. First sign of trouble and I'll be on you like a wolf on a chicken...

MOTHER-IN-LAW

You lived in a semi in Bridgford. Your mum was a teacher. When did YOU get to become such a dick? Twat.

Mother-in-law leaves Carmen

CARMEN

How dare you?! Rude.

Marrying the Wrong Kind

Ben walks into his ex's engagement party uninvited. His ex's fiancé has been blackmailing him. He wants to protect her, because she doesn't know what's really going on, and thinks he is just jealous.

BEN

I warned you to stay away from her! You only asked her to marry you so you can get your hands on my money.

BRIDE-TO-BE

Ben?! What the hell is going on!

BEN

He's been blackmailing me! This whole thing is about Billy's trust fund!

BRIDE-TO-BE

And you expect me to believe that?

BEN

I can prove it Becks. I was waiting to see what type of man he is.

GROOM

Come on then!

The groom turns Ben around and punches him.

BRIDE-TO-BE

Alan! Ben, please! Just leave it! Ben!

GROOM

Come on then! Come on! Let's have it! Big man! Come on!

BRIDE-TO-BE

Ben! Please just leave it!

GROOM

Fucking let's have it! Pussy!

Ben punches the groom.

BRIDE-TO-BE

Alan!

She goes to the groom's aid.

Somebody call an ambulance!

Dealer Dad

Oliver is a cocky, privileged drug dealer. He feels he's untouchable because he thinks he can talk his way out of anything. He's at a party selling MDMA cut with bath salts.

CLUBBER

What are these shit pills you sold me? What are these shit pills you sold me?!

OLIVER

Fuck off

Clubber walks off, annoyed at him. Oliver answers his phone.

OLIVER *Into his phone.*

Ellie? Your waters have broken? Are you sure? Yeah, yeah tell me. I'll be there ten minutes max. I love you too.

Oliver hangs up and approaches the exit. There's a police officer there. He turns swiftly to another exit. There are more police officers.

OLIVER

Fuck!

SCENE CHANGE OPTIONAL

Oliver is being pressed against the wall by a police officer.

OLIVER

What are you doing? You haven't seen shit! You haven't seen shit!

POLICE OFFICER

You need to come with me, alright? We've got footage of you cutting MDMA with bath salts.

OLIVER

Right! Right! I did it, I did it. I'll tell you what you want to know. But I've got to go.

POLICE OFFICER

Where?

OLIVER

My missus just rang. She's giving birth right now. Look in my back pocket. Look at my phone.

The police officer checks Oliver's phone. As he does, his radio goes off.

Please. Please. I've told her I'll be there.

Radio goes again.

POLICE OFFICER

Okay fine. We'll get there before we get to the station. All right?

OLIVER

Thank you. Thank you.

POLICE OFFICER

Come on.

Police officer moves him away from the wall and towards exit.

OLIVER

Where's Tesco? Can we get some nappies?

POLICE OFFICER

Oh, shut up.

Dealer Dad Two

Philip is a no-nonsense cop with a heart of gold. He is aggressively trying to force Oliver out of the party room and read him his rights.

PHILIP

We've got footage of you doing it! Bath salts in the MDMA you made!

OLIVER

I didn't do it!

Philip's colleague leaves them alone.

OLIVER

Alright. Alright. I did it. I did it. I'll tell you everything you want to know but I've got to go.

PHILIP

Go where?

OLIVER

My missus just rang me. She just rang. She's giving birth, right now. Please, I've got to go, I've told her I'll be there.

Look in my back pocket, look at my phone. It's got everything you want to know.

PHILIP

What's your code?

OLIVER

0000

Philip unlocks the phone.

OLIVER

Yeah, okay, go on the pictures. Mate, next one over, next one over!

PHILIP

That one?

OLIVER

Fuck off mate! Yes, next one over! Please.

PHILIP

How far gone is she?

OLIVER

Eight and a half months, only she's giving birth now!

PHILIP

I know what you're going through, mate. My missus is expecting too. I know how you feel.

OLIVER

Please. Please. I told her I'll be there.

PHILIP

Okay, fine. We'll pass by the hospital on the way to the station.

OLIVER

Thank you.

PHILIP

Come on.

Not the Blue

Carrie is the sister of the bride-to-be. The bride is stressing out and Carrie offers advice.

HARPER

So, I've done that... so umm I've got these two napkins... I've just got so much to sort out. So, I'm fifty-six for the...

CARRIE

Okay! Calm down! Okay. Stop stop stop. Sit down. No one gives a shit about what the napkins look like. I mean, all they're going to do is wipe their mouths with them. You know if you really want to look like you know what you're doing...I say...have everything mismatched.

HARPER

Mismatched?

CARRIE

Yeah! It's different! It's on trend! It's unique! Yeah, it's in style! Yeah? Right?

HARPER

Look. Why don't I just show you my dress okay? So, this is what I'll be wearing for my engagement party.

Carrie starts to laugh.

CARRIE

Har…Harper you can't wear blue! It looks shit. You know this, blue doesn't suit you. Right? Sorry! Sorry Harper I'm sorry! I'm sorry. I didn't mean to…I didn't mean to go that far.

HARPER

Everyone in that shop said I look great!

CARRIE

Yeah…they want you to be happy. But not as much as I want you to be happy. Mum's not here. And I'm trying to do her job. It's hard. It's really hard.

HARPER

Okay.

CARRIE

Right. These napkins. Okay, take one away. How do you feel?

HARPER

I think that one.

CARRIE

This one? Oh my gosh right. Guest list, come on let's go. Who's on it?

HARPER

Right so, so far…are you sure I look shit in blue?

CARRIE

Yeah…you're not wearing that. You're not…you're not wearing that. Sorry!

The Grope

Cooper is at a party, sitting next to him is a man with a party popper. He pops it, startling Cooper.

MAN

So, you're a law student, you play that ukulele…and you're averagely good-looking.

COOPER

Triple threat, what can I say.

MAN

And single?

COOPER

Why? You interested?

MAN

Is that a yes?

COOPER

Yes, I'm single, although my ex was a bit of a…how can I say…complete and utter wanker? So I'm not really too eager to jump back into the whole dating thing.

MAN

Who said anything about dating?

COOPER

Haha! Look, if I'm completely honest I've only ever been with one person. I'm new to this.

MAN

I think you're overthinking your honour, besides I'm pretty sure I've seen you on Grindr…

COOPER

Oh, I've been clocked! Okay uhm, yeah, I was on Grindr briefly but dick pics and married men isn't really quite what I'm looking for so…there's so many weirdos out there.

MAN

I'm not a weirdo…besides, what got you into law?

COOPER

Well, obviously I saw a matinee of Legally Blonde and it just naturally progressed from there.

MAN

You're joking, right?

COOPER

My dad's a lawyer. Wants me to carry the family name or some shit. Although now I think about it, I definitely went as Judge Judy for Halloween one year.

MAN

I should get your number anyway. You know…in case I run into any legal trouble.

He places his hand on Cooper's leg. Cooper throws his hand back.

COOPER

What are you doing?

MAN

I thought we had a moment? Sorry I...

COOPER

No, it's not you. I think I have a problem with intimacy. Why am I telling you this? Look uhm, sorry, I'm sorry, why don't I give you my number and we can go for a drink together? Another time, just you and me?

MAN gets up to leave.

MAN

Nah, forget it. A bit too much baggage.

COOPER

You don't need to be a prick about it.

MAN leaves.

COOPER

Seriously? Sorry that non-consensual groping doesn't do it for me! Jesus!

Bridal Jitters

At an engagement party, the bride-to-be, Bryony, is having second thoughts and asks her friend for help.

BRYONY

I need your help. Be honest with me. Me and Mike will be good together? Be honest, tell me honestly.

FRIEND

Okay, what's going on?

BRYONY

I don't think I can do it. I don't think I can marry him.

FRIEND

What?!

BRYONY

Don't get me wrong, you know he's so amazing. And he treats me so well and he's so sweet…and caring. He's like… he's like my best friend. You know? But I keep thinking about…and I know you're going to shout at me for this but…it's Josh.

FRIEND

Jesus! Josh is in prison now.

BRYONY

What?

FRIEND

Yeah, I think he got like twelve years for like flashing in the street.

BRYONY

Twelve years for…

FRIEND

Yeah.

BRYONY

Twelve years?!

FRIEND

Yeah! I wasn't…

BRYONY

How did I not know about this? Oh god, flashing in the street? You know, actually that doesn't surprise me in the slightest given what he was like back then. God. That's just put everything into perspective; just made it so much clearer. Thank you! That's been a great help. Okay. I'm going to go find Mike!

Baby Talk

Kristina is vivacious, defensive and makes snap decisions that are often influenced by her own self-loathing. She comes back from the toilet with a pregnancy test. She's a bit drunk. She shows it to the person she's just been talking to at the party.

KRISTINA

Two lines. That's means I'm pregnant, doesn't it? Will you check?

She hands it to her friend who nods.

The alcohol can't make a difference can it? You know, put another line on it? What am I going to do? Tell me what to do. It's not Kieran's. Kieran's gay. We were never even together. You won't tell my mum, will you?

FRIEND

No, I…

KRISTINA

It's Ian's.

FRIEND

What?!

KRISTINA

Ian, our boss! He probably hasn't been to a party in twenty years. His wife won't let him out! Do you think he'll fire me when he finds out? That asshole. He might try! I need this job. Twenty-two interviews I had before he took me on. He might make me have an abortion. Do you think he'll do that? I think I want this baby. What should I do?

FRIEND

Wow. Everyone in the office thought he was firing blanks, cos he had the snip last year.

KRISTINA

What?!

Studio Space

Danielle is usually easy-going, creative and charismatic, but she's in the middle of a long-running dispute with her neighbours and can't help but moan about it to a guy she's just met at a party.

DANIELLE

The Housing Association have told me I can't sing in my own home. The neighbours have complained. Apparently, it's anti-social. I'm a professional singer. This is how I make my living. So by making it a legal requirement that I have to stop practising, they're stopping me from doing my job. What am I supposed to do? I can't afford studio space.

PARTY GUY

You didn't say you were a singer! Sing something for me?

Danielle grins at him. She pulls him closer to her and sings softly in his ear.

Oh my god. You have a such a sexy voice.

DANIELLE

Thank you!

PARTY GUY

You can come and sing in my house any time. I kind of have this small studio set-up...nothing fancy, but you'd be welcome.

DANIELLE

Shut up! Really?

Hens

Phoebe walks up to her friends who are all whispering at a party. They go quiet when she gets close.

PHOEBE

What? What is it? Are you talking about Maria again? She looks so trash!

FRIEND 1

Yeah, right.

Phoebe takes a seat with them.

PHOEBE

I was thinking we could all get matching logos for the backs of our jackets for the hen party? Proper 80s American cheerleader vibe. I can sew them on if you like. I don't mind.

FRIEND 2

You're not coming to the hen party.

PHOEBE

Why not?

FRIEND 1

You've been uninvited. Sorry, I don't make the rules.

PHOEBE

Kirsty hasn't said anything to me...but she was a bit...what have I done? Do you know? That bitch! Wait, don't tell her I said that. If this is about her dress again, I already explained about it. It'll be okay, won't it? Oh. I don't know what to do...

Friend 2 starts filming her.

FRIEND 2

Phoebe's meltdown!

PHOEBE

Screw you. All of you.

Too Posh to Imprison

Tony is a security guard at a party, trying to stop a drunk guy from making a nuisance of himself.

TONY

Do me a favour and keep it in your pants, pal.

PARTY GUEST

What?!

TONY

You heard me. You carry on like that and we've got a consent issue. She's off her tits but the one thing she's been clear about is that she doesn't want to be around you! So off you fuck.

PARTY GUEST

Who the hell do you think you are?

TONY

Don't.

PARTY GUEST

That's it? 'Don't.' Where did Kerry find you eh? It sure as hell wasn't anywhere legit, was it? What are you? Ex-con?

Watches reaction, touches a nerve.

You are! You're one of Kerry's projects! How sweet! I think you'll find out here in the real world, people are free to do what they please…

The party guest turns back to the woman he's bothering. Tony springs into action and pins him to the ground with an elbow against the guy's throat.

TONY

I got put away by an over-privileged piece of shit like you. I was the fall guy for a rapist too posh to imprison. Wrong time. Wrong place. I'm not going to make the same mistake again.

Tent Peg

Tanya is at a party trying to tell a co-worker something confidential against a public backdrop, with loud music playing.

TANYA

Ssh! Keep it to yourself, okay? I don't want somebody hearing us and then calling the police before we've figured out what to do…

CO-WORKER

Let's go outside then.

TANYA

No, I want to keep an eye on her. Oh god. I don't know. Do you think she's lying?

They both look over at another woman. The co-worker shrugs.

The thing is, if we call the police and there's some guy she's killed lying in her flat, we're automatically going to get called in as witnesses. I've done it before. It's horrible. The whole case becomes about you. I'll get accused of collusion or something, because…and she doesn't know this…I was in the shop buying fags, when she rushed in and made her big declaration, 'I've done something terrible!'. And I didn't do anything then. I just left and came straight here. So of course, obviously nobody in the shop wants to get involved either. Because here she is and a few drinks in, I stupidly ask her if she's okay and she confesses everything. He was our college lecturer. I always thought he was alright, but apparently he took secret nudie photos of her…she stabbed him through the heart with a metal tent peg…! You've got to help me. Say I was with you all night, from your flat to here.

CO-WORKER

But you and I never met before today. I can't say that. It would be lying.

The woman looks at something out of shot, gets up and runs over to them.

WOMAN

The police are here. I'm really sorry Tanya, but I'm going to tell them you did it.

TANYA

What? You can't! I didn't!

WOMAN

I don't want to go to jail.

TANYA

Neither do I. And I haven't done anything. You bitch.

Her Song

Hannah is singing at an engagement party. She finishes her song and walks off the stage. She is a lesbian but hasn't come out to anyone yet. Her best friend thinks she has a crush an on old school friend, Gareth, who comes up to her after she's finished her song.

GARETH

That was amazing! You have such a good voice.

HANNAH

Thanks. That's really kind of you.

GARETH

Do you, um, want to dance?

HANNAH

No thanks. I'm rubbish at dancing.

Gareth turns away, not sure what to do.

FRIEND

Er...what the hell are you doing? You've had a crush on Gareth since you were, like, seven!

HANNAH

Yeah, but I feel like I'm on display. What if I did something wrong? I can't…just can't… there'll be other chances.

FRIEND

No there won't! And now Mia's coming over. You know what she's like.

HANNAH

(*Dreamily looking at Mia*) Yeah.

MIA approaches.

MIA

If you're not into him, mind if I have a go?

HANNAH

You can dance with me if you like, Mia. I mean…if Gareth's not interested. Although he probably is. Why wouldn't he be? You look gorgeous tonight by the way…really gorgeous.

FRIEND

Hannah?! Oh my god! Are you gay?

Tarot

Liz is doing a tarot card reading at her daughter's engagement party, when her daughter, Stacy, runs into the room and interrupts.

LIZ

Stacy, what's up?

STACY

Mum! I asked you not to do this. It's embarrassing. This is my night and I don't believe in that stuff.

LIZ

You might not but loads of people find it really helpful! And thanks a lot for your confidence in me. Fifteen years I've been doing this...

STACY

Please Mum!

LIZ

Okay...okay. Sorry. I'll put the cards away.

She starts to put them away, but the person who was in the middle of a reading stops her. She's upset. Mother and daughter look at her in surprise. She points to the death card which is lying face up as part of the spread the mother has done for her.

TAROT RECIPIENT

Don't. Not until you tell me what this means. Am I going to be alright? You can't just leave without telling me…

LIZ

Aw love. The death card is nothing to worry about. It signifies a new beginning. You made the right choice about your girlfriend. What she was doing to you…that's psychological abuse. Nobody has to put up with that, but she had a strong hold on you. Sometimes it feels like we need permission to move on, and that's what this card is giving you. You're going to be okay, do you hear? You're going to be okay.

TAROT RECIPIENT

Is it weird that this has made me feel…better? I feel sort of stronger. Like I'm not going to put up with her shit anymore. Thank you!

The girl hugs Liz and leaves.

STACY

Wow, we've been telling her that for years. Mum, (*long pause*) um, do you think I could have a reading?

LIZ

Sweetie!!!! I'd be honoured. Have a seat, love.

Funerals

The Dead Good Brothers

Brothers Chris and Ashley discuss their dodgy dealings at a relative's funeral.

CHRIS

I'm not sure I believe you. 20,000 units straight from mainland China at cost. What do you mean he said no?

ASHLEY

He said no, innit.

CHRIS

Well, they're not dodgy.

ASHLEY

I told him that but…

CHRIS

And exactly how did you tell him that?

ASHLEY

I…I said they're legit, here's the paperwork. Y'know, like you told me.

CHRIS

For god's sake, I don't believe this!!

ASHLEY

You're going mad, aren't you?

CHRIS

I'm stressing, yeah.

ASHLEY

Don't get stressed.

CHRIS

You're stressing me out!

ASHLEY

I'm taking the mick.

CHRIS

You what?

ASHLEY

I'm just winding you up, aren't I?

CHRIS

What? So, he's going to buy it?

ASHLEY

I'm just having you on, you dickhead.

CHRIS

Oh my god, that's…that's a hundred and twenty grand!

ASHLEY

Yeah.

CHRIS

Timing kiddo. Telling me at Grandad's bloody funeral!

Chris starts singing.

We're in the money. We're in the money…

ASHLEY

Hey…shush!

CHRIS

Yeah, but we did it! Nah, that's dead good!

WOMAN

Excuse me!

CHRIS

Sorry! Not dead good. Dead bad. Dead bad. Death is bad. Obviously. Oh, but you know you've just got to laugh haven't you? Eh? It's what the old man would have wanted. That and a pint. 'Ere, shall we have a beer?

ASHLEY

Yeah.

Both men simultaneously open their cans of beer and look to the sky.

CHRIS

Cheers Grandad! Let's get pissed.

Nuts about You

Evie thinks getting together with Matt is a done deal. She feels confident she can flirt with him, even at a funeral. In fact, she can't stop herself. She's a woman on a mission.

EVIE

Hey Matt.

MATT

Hi, you okay?

EVIE

Yeah, I'm okay thank you.

MATT

Uh?

Offers a cigarette

EVIE

No, I'm alright thanks uhm, so…uhm, oh fuck it. You and me. How about it?

MATT

Yeah, look, with everything that's been going on with the funeral and the scheduling stuff, I just don't think it's the right time for us to…

EVIE

Don't do this to me again, Matt! Not again. Everyone told me to just go for it. 'Yeah, it's a funeral, but when else are you going to see him?' It hurt enough last time. Was nuts about you and you knew it. You kissed me. I'm so stupid… just fuck off. Stay away from me.

She starts to walk away.

MATT

No look just…just wait…just wait, look…I was going to say yes to you and me but obviously with the funeral and stuff I just didn't think it was the right thing to do…

EVIE

Have I fucked it up?

MATT

No. No of course you've not! Come here

Matt and Evie hug.

EVIE

Come on…let's go.

They walk off, holding hands.

Dad

Nervous Izzy is talking to her sister at their father's funeral.

SISTER

I'm just worried about you. With Dad gone you're going to be in the house all alone.

IZZY

I can't stay in the house without Dad. I don't know how the fuse box works. And there's this thing that happens… sometimes right…nobody's sure why…but the whole thing just trips out. D'you remember? Dad always jiggled one of the switches. I never watched him…come on, can't I just stay with you?

SISTER

I'd love you to, but…

IZZY

It's Kyle

SISTER

He needs an office as the bank have said its branches are closing

IZZY

But…but what if the fuses blow? Suppose I could get the candles out but then…but then what if we run out of matches? And here's another thing, right? I don't know how to make eggy bread! Dad did…it's so stupid My lasagne always comes out perfect but my eggy bread is really soggy!

SISTER

I can make eggy bread. Anytime you want and Kyle can show you how to fix the fuses. Anything else you want…we're just down the road. Aren't we?

IZZY

I just want Dad back.

SISTER

It's going to be okay.

Friendly Blackmail

Scott is a local celebrity who has had an indiscreet night of drugs. A desperate friend has come to see him after a funeral. She tries to blackmail him.

NANCY

Hey Scott!

SCOTT

Thanks for coming, I really appreciate it.

NANCY

Yeah, it was a good service.

SCOTT

Thank you.

NANCY

Yeah…your dad would have been really proud.

SCOTT

Thanks.

NANCY

Scott?

SCOTT

Yeah?

NANCY

Gets phone out and passes it to Scott.

Is this you? Mm…it is, isn't it? I need fifty grand.

SCOTT

Visibly shaken.

I thought I could trust you, mate. I thought we were friends, was that all fake?

NANCY

No. It's not personal.

SCOTT

Just cos a few people know who I am it doesn't mean I've got that kind of cash in my bank account.

NANCY

Haven't you?

SCOTT

Look, I've got a few grand saved up. You can have that. Once you've got it you can pay me back, yeah?

NANCY

I need fifty grand now. Or they're going to kill me. You know people. You can make this happen, because if you don't...I swear to God, I'm sharing this.

SCOTT

Fucking blackmail, Nance? Please. Please don't do this, Nance. It was a total one-off; I wasn't even supposed to be there! I'm being scouted for the England team, this'll ruin that! They'll kick me off the Notts team too. Please! Nancy, please!

NANCY

Scott. You've got twenty-four hours.

Nancy walks off leaving Scott.

SCOTT

Fuck.

Tough Crowd

Father Tim wanted to be an actor in his youth. Now he is a priest at the local church, where he's just performed a funeral. Here we find him approaching the daughter of the deceased.

FATHER TIM

My commiserations on your loss.

MOURNER

Thank you, Father.

FATHER TIM

The service, was it to your liking?

MOURNER

Yeah, it were lovely, thanks.

FATHER TIM

I'm so glad that I hit the right notes.

MOURNER

Yeah, it were what he would've wanted.

FATHER TIM

Oh, that's wonderful, but I expect he would've preferred a front row seat rather than a view from the box, so to speak.

MOURNER

Yeah, he did love theatre.

FATHER TIM

Oh! So do I! Romeo and Juliet. Gilbert and Sullivan. Jeeves and Wooster. The footlights, the smell of grease paint. Spellbinding. To be or not to be, that is the question. I do like to keep things light-hearted. There's no point in all this doom and gloom is there?

MOURNER

No. Well, anyway, we better be getting t'wake.

FATHER TIM

Well, off you go then. Have a good knees-up. I say, if you…if you get a spare moment can you put a review on the church website? It's Father Tim. Baptisms, weddings, funerals. Anything really, just the usual stuff.

Father Tim takes a deep breath.

Bloody. Tough. Crowd. Is that the time? Christ.

The Lunchtime Mix-Up

Quirky Mia is the vicar's assistant. She is attending the wake, uninvited, to find someone to fill in some paperwork. There has been an error. The wrong body has been cremated.

MIA

Could I have a word?

MOURNER

Yeah.

MIA

It's about the deceased. God rest his soul.

MOURNER

Oh…okay. Who are you?

MIA

I work with Father Hamilton in the church. I cremate the bodies, as it were, the switch. Oh. That sounds a bit creepy! (*Giggles*) What I mean is my role's more of a technical one, rather than spiritual. Does that make sense?

MOURNER

So, is there a problem?

MIA

Yes. Well, potentially. We've…we've cremated the wrong body.

MOURNER

What?

MIA

I thought it would be best if I come out and tell you in person, rather than over the phone or in an email…oh god. That sounds terrible. What I mean to say is…you know…

She starts to giggle

I'm so sorry. I always laugh when I get nervous. I'm not laughing at…

She pulls a piece of paper out of her pocket and reads a name from a list.

John!

MOURNER

So, where's John now?

MIA

Still in the hearse. He's parked outside. Never got unloaded. And I can't get him out until the paperwork's signed. So, are you able to sign it for me…?

MOURNER

Yes, yes...where is it?

Mia hands papers over.

MIA

Quickly though please. I start my lunch in five minutes.

MOURNER

John would have loved this.

MIA

Oh, that's great news. We aim to please! Do you think you could leave us a Google review? Oh! My Deliveroo! Thanks again! Thanks for your understanding and sorry for your loss.

Family Affairs

Connor, an affable, popular guy who is really stressed at work, is trying to gain control of his family life. He's drunk at a funeral. He stands out because he's dressed for clubbing and is talking loudly to his wife.

WIFE

It's a funeral for Christ's sake!

CONNOR

This stuff's designer. Your dad would have appreciated it. Rich old bastard…

Mourners start looking around at him.

WIFE

Shhhh.

CONNOR

Raising his voice.

It needs to be said. He was a bastard. And you lot don't even know the half of it. We got half his estate. That's how guilty he was feeling about her.

Connor gestures towards his wife.

MOURNER

Who are you?

WIFE

Connor, don't!

CONNOR

Who am I? I don't think you're qualified to ask that question my friend, but I'm going to answer it anyway…

WIFE

No!

The whole room is looking now.

CONNOR

I'm Phoebe's husband. Phoebe was John's daughter.

Looks at John's son.

That's right, mate. She's your sister from another mother. Literally. John had a whole second family that none of you knew anything about, a family that's grieving just as hard as you are right now. Although I'm not grieving. I think he was a prick. Let's just say, me and him didn't share a moral compass. I love my wife. She's cleverer than me. Always wanted to be a solicitor but ended up as a secretary. It hurts her to this day that John chose to send his other kids to uni, despite them being thick as pig shit.

JOHN'S SON

GET OUT!

WIFE

I can't believe you're doing this! *(To John's wife)* I didn't want any trouble.

She starts to cry and walk out. Connor goes to grab her. He's distraught.

CONNOR

It needed to be said. It's not fair. Why should we have to live in the shadows, always watching our step, just because of the shitty decisions your dad made? Please don't cry.

JOHN'S WIFE

He's right. It's not fair. I know John had his secrets. It's only right that you should meet his family…

John's wife smiles in a kindly way at Connor's wife, who smiles back. Connor runs over to hug John's wife and starts crying.

CONNOR

Thank you. Thank you. She won't say it but it's all she's ever wanted; to know her grandparents and uncles and aunties…

Worst Day Ever

Shona is blackmailing Paige (spontaneous, heart-on-her-sleeve, self-confidence problems). She knows Paige slept with the deceased and has been demanding money to keep quiet about it. Now she wants a big pay-off, otherwise she's going to announce it at the funeral, in front of the family and the deceased's wife.

SHONA

You slept with him, didn't you?

PAIGE

What? Come off it. He's married.

SHONA

I know you did. Because he told me. We were close you know. He showed me the letters you sent an' all.

PAIGE

You've got it wrong.

SHONA

Then you won't mind if I send those letters to his wife.

PAIGE

What do you want?

SHONA

Grand a month.

PAIGE

Fuck off. I haven't got that sort of money. Can't give it to you if I haven't got it, can I?

SHONA

That's not my problem.

PAIGE

This is fucked up. I loved him. More than she ever did. She didn't get him at all. This is the worst day of my life and here you are trying to profit from my grief. Have you ever lost anyone? You ever lost your soulmate? Because believe me...

SHONA

Oh enough! Spare me the sob story. The first instalment's due at the end of the week.

PAIGE

You stupid bitch! What have I ever done to you?

Paige gets up and starts a fight with Shona.

SHONA

It's not about me, honest! It's about what you've done to her!

Gestures towards the wife. Paige looks regretful.

Killed by Bears

Desperate and defensive Daz fancies Stacey, but he's worried his disability will put her off. He's shy and nervous. However, when he makes a joke, Stacey laughs. Feeling encouraged, Daz goes for it.

DAZ

Is it weird that they've got so many sweets at a funeral?

STACEY

(*Laughing*) Do you think they should have more serious food?

DAZ

Maybe!

Encouraged by her laughter Daz chucks some gummy bears at his mouth and misses.

You know if I choke on one of these things, I want my obituary to say I was killed by bears…

STACEY

(*Laughing harder*) You're funny. Have we met before?

DAZ

Yeah. At Carol's 70th. Don't you remember? There was a bunch of us outside at the end, playing spin-the-bottle. Kids games. But it was a laugh. We kissed. You and me. It was magic. I couldn't stop thinking about it. This is a bit embarrassing but I wrote a poem about you. Stacey, I don't suppose you'd...

Stacey gets up.

STACEY

You know my name? I don't remember you at all! This is too weird. I'm sorry but I think you've got the wrong person.

She walks off.

DAZ

I haven't.

A guy who has been watching the conversation walks over to him.

EAVESDROPPER

Bit of overkill with the poem mate. Made you look needy!

DAZ

Who the fuck asked you?

Not a Fucking Charity

Josh is the local stoner (laid-back, polite, slightly shy but in a charming way). He sits watching the funeral guests unhappily. A guy comes over to him.

GUY

Josh mate, you got any gear on you?

JOSH

Yeah.

GUY

Can I have some? A little pick-me-up? This is depressing!

JOSH

Alright, but don't take it all.

Josh takes a bag out of his pocket and hands it to the guy.

GUY

Cheers pal.

The guy takes the bag and leaves.

A woman comes over. She sits next to Josh.

WOMAN

So sad, isn't it?

JOSH

Yeah.

WOMAN

Can I...?

She makes a smoking gesture.

JOSH

Fuck's sake. I'm not a charity!

The woman gives him a pleading gesture.

JOSH

Tony's got my gear. He just went outside.

WOMAN

Thanks, hun. I owe you!

Older man comes over to Josh.

OLDER GUY

What the fuck are you doing, dealing at my brother's funeral?

JOSH

I'm not dealing. I'm not a dealer. I was trying to help them. They were sad.

The guy grabs Josh.

GET OFF ME!

OLDER GUY

I know who you are. Always been a useless waste of space…and now this!

They hear a siren. Josh struggles to get away.

JOSH

Hey, no. It's a misunderstanding. That gear was for personal use. Please mate. You got to believe me. I didn't even want to give it to them…

Seize the Day

The emotion of the day has got to Poppy, who is sad, depressed, lovable but in need of a hero. A male friend is comforting her.

POPPY

Don't look at me. I'm a mess. I can't help it. I loved him so much and now he's gone. I'm crying, like, all the time. All those weeks he was in hospital. I visited him every day, but do you know what we talked about? Oh my god. I feel so bad about this. I went on and on about how shit things are at work. It wasn't fair on him. And he was in so much pain. But I couldn't stop myself. He's always been there for me. So I just waffled on and on about Clare in the office and how she's always trying to pitch my ideas to Nathan, and then about how I fell out really badly with Kelly, that's my cousin. We were always so close. I know that upset him. He's always treated Kelly like a daughter. I don't know. When I think about what I should have said. I should have been making his final few hours better, happier…

FRIEND

I'm sure he was glad you were there with him. (*Pause*) Hey, did you hear what his first choice of song for the funeral was? *Who Let the Dogs Out?!*

POPPY

No!

Poppy starts to laugh.

FRIEND

It's true. He was adamant and he was only doing it to annoy Keith. Your mum talked him out of it.

POPPY

Thank god for that!

FRIEND

You've got such a nice laugh! Poppy, this is the wrong place for this, but I don't know when I'm going to see you again. Do you want to go out for a drink sometime?

POPPY

Yes! Yes, I'd really like that.

Prison

Bending the Rules

Pete's a kind, thoughtful man, who wishes he could have been confident in his profession like his brother, rather than resort to fraud in order to maintain his flashy image.

BROTHER

Ay up jailbird!

PETE

Come to gloat, have we? What you here for?

BROTHER

See why you did it.

PETE

You wouldn't understand.

BROTHER

Try me.

PETE

It's complicated.

BROTHER

If you needed money, why didn't you ask me?

PETE

I didn't need the money.

BROTHER

Why then?

PETE

They make me see a therapist. She reckons it stems from my relationship with Dad. You know, to try and impress him? Like you'd understand.

BROTHER

Well, you've fucked that now.

PETE

I know. I know. I really fucked up. But I'm going to make it up to him, as soon as I get out of here.

Brother laughs

Straight job. No bending the rules this time.

BROTHER

Bending the rules?

PETE

And I'll get Fiona to give me back joint custody of Jake. Will you tell him that? Will you tell him for me please?

BROTHER

Are you joking?

PETE

Please Ross. I'm not…I'm not safe here. I need to get moved. And I need you to talk to Dad to get him to vouch for me in my transfer appeal.

BROTHER

We had the national newspapers round.

PETE

Please Ross! If I stay in here…I will die in here. Do you know what it's like to be pinned down by four guys? And then a fifth guy unbuttoning himself…or pissing in the corner of your bunk because it's too dangerous for you to be up at night…so please talk to Dad. He listens to you. Please just… promise me you'll…you'll talk to him. He listens to you.

BROTHER

I'll see what I can do.

PETE

Thank you! Thank you, Ross.

BROTHER

No promises.

PETE

Thank you, Ross.

BROTHER

Look…I'll try. No promises.

PETE

Please…

The Plea

Easy-going criminal lawyer, Kash, has come to talk to Peter to discuss his plea in court.

KASH

You alright Peter?

Kash sits opposite Peter.

Right, I've got parents' evening to go to so I'm going to get straight to it. Did you do it?

Kash holds up a hand to silence him.

Before you answer that, I think you should know that…

He gets evidence out of his briefcase.

I've seen the CCTV footage of you shredding the paper evidence. The hard drives that you thought you deleted; you've not deleted them. The police also have an eyewitness, they will disclose that to me later so…did you do it?

PETER

No comment.

KASH

I'm not a copper. I'm your solicitor.

PETER

Not guilty.

KASH

Peter, if you plead guilty you'll get one maybe two years, maybe come out earlier for good behaviour. But if you don't and it drags out to court and you put it in the hands of a judge…then you will go down for ten maybe twelve years. Is that what you want? Ten or twelve years of you looking at these walls with your hand over your arsehole? As your solicitor, I would advise you to plead guilty.

PETER

Okay.

KASH

Good. I'll have a statement drafted for you and signed officially tomorrow but for now if I can get you to sign that…good. Guard! We'll have this matter resolved for you very quickly. A lighter sentence for sure. And Peter? Whatever you do…don't pick up that soap.

Sisterly and Brotherly Love

Kerry goes to confront her brother in prison to tell him that she is ashamed of him and won't cover for him anymore.

BROTHER

Don't shout at me.

KERRY

Shout at you, course I'm going to fucking shout at you! You're a fucking arsehole. You didn't tell me you stole a car, never mind burned it. Of all the stupid shit you've done, this is the one that's confused me the most. You were the only one in the car, weren't you?

Silence from the brother.

I knew it. Who was with you? Who was with you? Who?!

BROTHER

Pete.

KERRY

Pete?! What?

BROTHER

He said if I didn't do it he was going to shank me up.

KERRY

Oh Jesus Christ.

BROTHER

Kerry, I'm scared. I wasn't meant to get caught.

KERRY

Well, duh…

BROTHER

He's been sending me messages. He said if I tell anyone anything…then he's going to…

KERRY

Yeah, of course he is! He's Pete! You're an idiot. You've left me, ain't you? To sort it out again. It's always me coming back here, isn't it? Watching you in those grey sweatpants. I'm fed up with it.

BROTHER

What am I meant to do now?

KERRY

Well, I've got to fucking sort it out now ain't I? Eh? Me. Look, come here. I don't know how. Yeah? But I'll get it sorted, yeah?

She grabs his hand.

PRISON OFFICER

No touching.

KERRY

Oh sorry…

Kerry drops her hold on her brother.

BROTHER

Thank you. I love you.

KERRY

I know. I love you too.

Prison Payback

Kezza has been ambushed by another inmate who believes she needs to hand out her own punishment for the crimes committed. After visiting is over, Kezza is trapped in a room with her.

KEZZA

Uh, excuse me? Still in here! Oi! Guard! Bastard.

INMATE

I heard you're getting out of here next week.

KEZZA

Yeah.

INMATE

Don't think you're going to have it easy. I got people on the outside waiting for you.

KEZZA

Really?

INMATE

I think you're going to have an accident soon. Yeah?

KEZZA

You've had it in for me since day one. What the fuck is your problem?

INMATE

You sold roofies didn't you?

KEZZA

Among other things, yeah, so what?

INMATE

My sister was spiked.

KEZZA

So, what do you want me to do? Say I'm sorry?

The inmate attacks Kezza, slamming her into a wall.

INMATE

Sorry?! You need a taste of your own medicine. Take it now.

The inmate forces Kezza to swallow pills.

Take it. Swallow. Good girl. Open up. Open up.

She checks Kezza's mouth.

Good girl. Guards?

The door opens and the inmate leaves. Kezza immediately spits out the pills and swears at the guard.

The Suspect

Liz has just witnessed the suicide of her cell mate and is being interviewed by the police. Liz thinks she's answering questions about her cell mate's state of mind, so is astonished to learn she's about to get the blame.

POLICE INTERVIEWER

Right Liz, take your time, and in your own words, tell us what you saw.

LIZ

She was just hanging there, not breathing.

POLICE INTERVIEWER

Did you attempt first aid?

LIZ

No. Why are you asking me that?

POLICE INTERVIEWER

Liz, we found your fingerprints on her body and on the light fitting. Do you know why that might be?

LIZ

What?! What are you trying to say? I didn't touch her. I found her.

POLICE INTERVIEWER

You two didn't get on, did you?

LIZ

I'm here to tell you what happened when I found her. Am I a suspect?

POLICE INTERVIEWER

Tell us about the fingerprints. They were found around the tops of the arms and around her neck. Liz, I believe you murdered…

LIZ

That's a lie. Show me the fingerprints, show me the match.

POLICE INTERVIEWER

I can't do that…

LIZ

You should've been watching her around the clock. What the fuck?! I can't do your jobs for you! You fucking prick! Get my solicitor in here now. Get my fucking rep in here now!

I Have Rights

Inmate Shane is confident he can sweet talk the prison counsellor into giving him the diagnosis of poor mental health that will prevent him from going back into the general population of the prison.

THERAPIST

Good morning, Shane, how are you?

SHANE

Well, I guess you're the therapist, you tell me.

THERAPIST

Well, today we're completing your assessment, and I wondered what you wanted to add to it?

SHANE

I don't know. Depression? Anxiety? Sleepless nights, constant threats. Suicidal thoughts, just not coping. I trust you'll make the right decision.

THERAPIST

Shane, I think you have adjusted remarkably well. My recommendation is now that you are transferred from the isolation wing to the general population.

SHANE

What? You can't do that. You can't put me back in there! I'm a dead man! They'll kill me! Or worse.

THERAPIST

Sorry Shane, I can't help you anymore.

SHANE

You can't do this! I have rights! I have protection rights, you fucking bitch! You can't do this you, fucking bitch!

Stitched Up

Maggie has stitched up someone else to do time instead of her. She visits them to gloat, but the mood changes when she discovers that she hasn't been as careful as she thinks she has.

MAGGIE

You look in a good mood. I didn't expect that.

INMATE

What, because you stitched me up, you mean?

MAGGIE

Look, I know you're feeling really pissed off at the moment. But you know what? In six years' time, when you get out, you'll thank me.

INMATE

Oh yeah, why's that?

MAGGIE

When you get out, there'll be £300,000 waiting for you. That's if you're a good girl.

INMATE

And will I get my money when I get out tomorrow?

MAGGIE

You're being very optimistic!

INMATE

You dropped a hairclip. It doesn't match my DNA. My solicitor's got a few odds and ends to sort out but I expect to be out of here very soon.

MAGGIE

I'm too old to go to prison, and if I go down and you get out? Just keep looking over your shoulder.

A prison guard calls time on visiting and Maggie leaves.

For Callum

Prisoners are leaving the prison visiting room. The guard leaves too. Antony and Rob are left behind. Rob has paid off the guard to leave them in the room together.

ANTONY

What the fuck's going on?

ROB

We are mates, aren't we? I mean you wouldn't keep secrets from me, would you?

ANTONY

No.

ROB

Don't take me for a fucking idiot. You know exactly what I mean. He's the one person in my life that I ever really cared about.

ANTONY

I ain't got time for this.

ROB

Shut the fuck up.

ANTONY

Guard?!

ROB

Shut the fuck up!

Rob launches at Antony in a frenzy and repeatedly stabs Antony with a homemade knife.

That was for Callum, you fucking prick!

Too Late Now

Lisa is pretending to be a lawyer. She is visiting a prisoner in the hope of scamming her out of her drug earnings.

LISA

I'm afraid Mr. Williams hasn't been entirely honest with you. Let's just say that he's been spending your money. But it's okay, that's why Mrs. Clark sent you to me. I've set up a bank account, the details are in there. You will need to change the password as soon as possible though, so only you can access it.

Inmate takes the information across and looks through it.

Now if you tell me the details of where the money is, I can put it in for you. That's no trouble at all. I do have other places to be today.

INMATE

You ain't no solicitor. I've got a mate in Holloway. You pulled the same shit there. Dealers talk, yeah. We got a network. You ain't getting your hands on our money.

LISA

Now hold on just a moment, I'm sure we can work something out here.

INMATE

Too late. You're fucking dead.

Lisa has a meltdown, begging for another chance as the inmate leaves the room.

Do-Gooder

Anti-drugs therapist Kris spots an opportunity to make the world a better place, only to be confronted with prejudice.

KRIS

Mike told me the guards are getting an eighty per cent cut on any narcotics you bring in here. That's why they turn a blind eye to the drones.

INMATE

It's none of your business.

KRIS

They are exploiting you. They are exploiting your contacts to make money illegally and each night, they go home to their lives as free men while you're stuck in here. And look at the damage it's causing. Half the guys in here are on crack. It's hardly helping their rehabilitation. I can get funding for a good cause. What do you say I cover your twenty per cent? You'll basically be helping me to help these poor fuckers clean up their act. It deserves a wage! What do you say?

INMATE

Nah.

KRIS

What do you mean no? You still get your money! It's win-win.

INMATE

Been here five minutes and think you know better than me! Fucking do-gooding twat. Never have liked your sort.

Kris pushes him up against the wall.

KRIS

Listen mate, I'm giving you a chance here. I'm trying to make the world a better place. And if I have to stop you bringing your poorly cut cheap-ass shit in here by going to the top, then I'll do that. You'll get 24-hour surveillance and your guard mates will find themselves on the other side of the bars. I wonder what they'll do to you then? Especially when I tell them it was you who grassed 'em up.

Mother's Boy

Shy, troubled Lee confronts his inmate mother for the first time since she was sentenced and discovers his voice at last.

LEE

Hello mum.

MUM

Hi baby boy! I knew you'd come and see me. Took your time though.

LEE

Yes, sorry.

MUM

I could've done with your support in court! That stupid cow ripped me to shreds. Why didn't you stick up for me?

LEE

Mum! Everything she said was true! I thought you were listening. You told me you'd changed. You told me you were going to try harder.

MUM

Why are you taking your sister's side? It's her lies that have put me in here.

LEE

You don't get it, do you? All my life, we've had to put up with you leaving us in the house on our own for weeks on end, bringing home boyfriends who hit us…and worse!

MUM

A little bruise maybe. It was nothing like what they did to me!

LEE

If you knew what they were capable of, then why did you let them near us, mum? We're your children.

MUM

You were always my favourite though!

LEE

I know that and as a kid, that's what kept me quiet. At least I didn't have it as bad as Emily. I was just trying to survive. You might not see it, but she's the same as you now. And it's your fault. I hope you rot in here. You deserve it.

Standing up for my Kids

Danielle is in a group therapy session in prison. She has a short fuse and a confrontational manner, but she's trying to be patient.

DANIELLE

What can I say? I'd do anything for my kids.

COUNSELLOR

But you'd been warned. If you got into another fight, the school would press charges. And here you are again. You knew that would happen. And you knew you wouldn't be able to look after your kids properly from in here...

DANIELLE

So what are you saying? That I'm not a good mum? That I don't love my kids? You're all the same. You only ever see one side of the story and it's never mine.

Danielle spits on the floor.

COUNSELLOR

Hey!

DANIELLE

Do you really think that I got myself locked up to escape my responsibilities? I got myself locked up because I was facing up to my responsibilities. That stupid cow, the school governor. Her lanky twat of a son has had it in for my Jayden since he started at that school and everyone; the teachers, the governor, the head, all turn a blind eye. My Jayden had the point of a knife pushed from here to here.

Danielle indicates chin to collar bone.

And when he complained, he was called a liar by his form tutor, who suggested perhaps he'd scratched himself on the bushes instead. Scratched himself on the bushes! Then she had the cheek to ask me to stop Jayden telling tales on her Ayaan. Yeah, I let her have it. Who else is going to stand up for my kids, except me? No one!

Therapy

In the Workplace

Lucy doesn't realise that she's been sent to group therapy because she has been accused of workplace bullying.

MAN

I bought them at 16p and I'm on a 4000% return now.

SECOND MAN

Cool.

COUNSELLOR

Good morning, everyone! How are we?

LUCY

So…why am I here again? I was told I only had to do one session. I signed that form you gave me. You've got the form, haven't you?

COUNSELLOR

Yes, yes, I've got the form, so Liz said…

LUCY

Wait, that's why I'm here? Because of that complaint Liz made about me? I passed her files onto her accounts for her. She was the one who forgot. In fact, I was doing her a favour. We've been over this. And yet I'm the one who's sat here in this therapy session? If you all had to sit in the office with Liz, you'd all raise your voices as well…Hang on a minute. Is that why I was here the first time as well? Oh. My. God. It was, wasn't it? Evil! I bet she said I was bullying her, didn't she? DIDN'T SHE? And you believe her. Bet you believe her. Bet you all believe her.

COUNSELLOR

Calm down, Lucy.

LUCY *(to the room)*

Screw you. Screw you and screw you.

COUNSELLOR

It wasn't Liz that referred you. She just wanted you to sign the form. You missed out a section, just that one…

Lucy signs form

COUNSELLOR

Thank you. Dom, how are we?

DOM

Since Afghanistan…been struggling, losing six men to an IED. It does take its toll on you. It's a nightmare to get back. When you wake up in the morning sweating…heart racing…any loud noises as well, that really triggers some bad memories.

Therapeutic Truth

In a group therapy session, Lila is shocked and upset to discover that what her childhood foster family had been doing to her amounted to abuse and that her upbringing was far from normal.

THERAPIST

Thank you for sharing that with us today, who'd like to go next? Lila, how about you?

LILA

Yeah.

THERAPIST

Tell us a bit about yourself. You were in foster care?

LILA

Yeah, I was in care for 10 years, but I don't like to feel sorry for myself. On those days you just sort of get on with it and move forward.

GROUP MEMBER

Yeah man, that's right!

LILA

Uh, my foster parents Ron and Lesley were nice enough. I had good meals. I could have a bath once a month…no I'm kidding. I could use the shower any time I wanted. You know and but yeah everything was fine.

THERAPIST

If everything was fine, why are you here today?

LILA

Right. This is going to sound stupid. But it's my boyfriend, Eddie. He's always overthinking stuff and when he gets an idea in his head, woe betide anyone who gets in his way. So, I came here to shut him up basically.

GROUP MEMBER

Sometimes you've gotta do that, y'know?

LILA

He keeps thinking maybe, you know, my foster parents were a bit weird. But everybody's a bit weird, aren't they, sometimes? Maybe I'm just weird. It's allowed, isn't it? So…

THERAPIST

So, in what way does your partner think Ron and Lesley were weird?

LILA

They were just really over-protective. I mean, you can understand it can't you? It's not your kid. I mean most parents are over-protective anyway. So sometimes they shut me in.

THERAPIST

In the house?

LILA

In a cupboard. It made sense. You know, it was so I didn't hurt himself when they went out and… I didn't mind, apart from when it was overnight, an' I got scared…and sometimes I would have my clothes off…

THERAPIST

Take a breath…it's okay…take a deep breath

LILA *(visibly upset, finally realising the truth of her past)*

Anyway…who's next?

Risking it All

A woman in an AA group describes her relapse.

WOMAN

So, Jenny, tell us about your date.

JENNY

So yeah, he's so fit. His name's Colin, and yeah, I've worked with him on and off for years and I've always fancied him. I mean, usually we'd meet in the day, have a coffee and discuss whatever project we're doing at the time and it was always flirty and full on. God, we're usually the loudest people in the room. He tries to make me laugh and I try to telepathically signal to him that he should lean across the table and kiss me. But he never does. Then all of a sudden, I'm in the pub waiting for him. Alcohol's involved. This has never happened. I wonder what he's going to tell his wife. So, I'm nervous. Of course I'm nervous.

WOMAN

It's okay.

JENNY

I have a drink. Dutch courage. And then he texts to say he's running late, but not to worry, there'll still be plenty of time to give me one in the disabled loos or… God, it's a weird fucking joke, isn't it? And it's not like him. I assume he's nervous too. Maybe something's going to happen. I want it to happen. So, I have another drink. And then another. And I do the usual trick with the lemon slices, y'know, to keep count. By the time he arrives there's fifteen lemon slices in my drink and I'm absolutely shitfaced. His beautiful and cute face is standing over me and he's helping me to my feet, but he's laughing. He's laughing and my face is burning. He thinks it's a one off. He thinks that nerves got the better of me. But he doesn't have a fucking clue, does he?

She starts to get angry.

He doesn't know that it's been nearly three years since I've been to a pub. And nearly three years since I've had a drink. He doesn't know how hard I've fought to resist, and how now, I have to start all over again. Three years in the bin, just because he was running fucking late. It's weird. I hate him, I fucking hate him for making me want him so badly I was willing to risk it all again. Willing to risk it for that fucking dickhead.

WOMAN

You are not the only one in this room who's been willing to risk it all.

JENNY

I mean I don't want to be back, I don't, just because of him. He's got a fucking wife and kids and…what am I doing? What am I doing? Anyway…that's me…who's next?

Taking the Piss

Ellie is in a new-age group therapy session to help her with her depression. She pours her heart out to them, not expecting their main tip to be to drink your own urine.

ELLIE

So, you know how the experts are always saying get more sleep? Thing is I was getting like fourteen hours a night! It makes sense though cos I was just being so mean to my boyfriend. I mean I was just chipping away at his ego. Thing is, it was all just to make me feel more in control. Like make his self-esteem so low that he wouldn't leave me. That backfired. But I've got a diagnosis now. And medication. But I thought getting some wellbeing therapy can't exactly hurt, can it? So that's why I'm here. It's lovely to meet you all.

GROUP LEADER

It's lovely to meet you too, Ellie. We're a very friendly group. May I ask, how long have you been drinking urine?

ELLIE

Wait! Urine? As in…piss? Drinking piss.

GROUP LEADER

Did you get the leaflet I sent you?

ELLIE

No. No, uhm…

GROUP LEADER

Not only does it whiten your teeth and brighten your eyes, it's actually really good for depression.

ELLIE

This is not CBT, then?

GROUP LEADER

No.

ELLIE

I have just given my whole life story.

GROUP LEADER

This is the Yellow Smiles Club.

ELLIE

Yellow Smiles Club.

Starts to laugh.

GROUP LEADER

Yes. Alright Ellie, you're amongst friends here. Why not give it a go?

GROUP MEMBER

It's so good for you!

ELLIE

It helps with depression?

GROUP LEADER

Absolutely.

ELLIE

Drinks a glass of urine.

It's quite nice.

Group applauds her.

It's alright. Yeah, refreshing, actually. Wasn't expecting it to be nice…and who… whose piss is this?

GROUP LEADER

It's mine.

ELLIE

Oh, zingy.

GROUP LEADER

Yes, I've been drinking rather a lot of lemonade recently.

ELLIE

Thanks for accepting me into the group.

GROUP LEADER

You're very welcome.

Group accept Ellie, glasses are raised.

ELLIE

Again? Okay… again.

She drinks.

Ahhhh…great.

Trigger

Maddie is wondering why she finds it difficult to answer the phone or speak to clients without having a panic attack.

COUNSELLOR

And what about you Maddie? Do those things happen to you?

MADDIE

I just let the phone ring and ring. Usually, if I do that, then usually someone else will pick it up. I've got really good at making myself look busy. And if a client asks for me by name, then I just have this whole list of excuses I can reel off so I don't actually have to talk to anyone. I mean I've actually managed to not answer the phone for about a month, or speak to anyone in the office, apart from my personal secretary, for I actually don't know how long. But it just means I'm now more terrified than ever to actually answer the phone.

COUNSELLOR

So, the phone, what triggers you?

MADDIE

I feel like I've actually spent weeks trying to work out what is wrong with me. Whole weeks. I don't know…nothing's changed. Uh, that's why I've been coming here. I was hoping that you could give me some tips on coping strategies on how to like get through it? Yeah? Cos that's what we're all here for…yeah? Right? So, anyone got anything? No? Cos I just…you know…I just…I'm getting a bit sick of coming here every week and just sitting. And smiling and nodding and helping each other but nothing's fucking changing. So, I need some concrete… something concrete cos I can't - I can't keep doing this.

COUNSELLOR

These things do take time. You know, one day at a time.

MADDIE

Yeah, one…one day at a time right. The thing is though uh this has been going on for quite a while and I've been coming to these sessions for, you know, for a few months now and everyone seems to want to really help each other and we all nod along and we all smile. Um but nothing's actually helping. Nothing's working. None of you have been able to give me anything to help me. No offence but neither have you and you're meant to be kind of leading the group so is someone going to tell me what the fuck I'm meant to do or is this it? We're just going to like leave? Go about our days, come back next week. Drink the same fucking shit coffee.

COUNSELLOR

Just calm down and just think a little.

MADDIE

I mean I actually think I am calm. I feel really fucking calm. I just need something to just change. And everyone's fucking looking at me like I'm an absolutely crazy person.

Maddie looks at one member of the group who is asleep.

Cool. Yep. Do you know what? Yeah? Fuck you. Fuck you. Certainly, fuck you. Fuck all of you. Especially fuck you. Yeah? Fucking waste of time this session. Yeah. Do you know what would be even better? Let's all just go get fucking high, yeah? Come back to the pub, let's get high. Fucking better spending my money on that than this shit. Feels much better as well. Fuck you all. Yeah? See you later, come on.

COUNSELLOR

We'll just give her a moment. Tom? Tom? Will somebody wake him up?

The Workplace Bully

An anxious IT professional is in a group therapy session, confessing to the incident that forced him to realise he needed therapy.

COUNSELLOR

You're definitely taking the right approach. Do you want to carry on?

IT GUY

As soon as I saw them walk out of Collin's office…I just knew they'd been talking about me. You know? I saw his face…and he just…you just know. He's been after the data lead position since I started. You know it was little things at first that he did like…chewing gum under my computer.

COUNSELLOR

Yeah, that's how it usually starts.

IT GUY

You know, things like finding sexy love letters from Bella in finance, who I sort of have a thing for…but they weren't from her. Finding porn on my screen when I went to the loo and then everyone sees it in the office. That sort of thing. Childish. I don't have any proof of them doing this. I still don't. But I didn't need it and I knew it was them. The air gun was in my bag and I was holding onto it for a friend's dad because there are some rabbits being shot in Colwick? Anyone know about this? No? Uhm, it was just it was just so easy. I put my hand in my bag and my finger found the trigger instantly. Next thing I knew I just pulled it out and pressed it into his forehead.

COUNSELLOR

It's okay. You're in a safe place.

IT GUY

When they pulled me away I...I saw I left a red mark on his forehead. He was crying. Shaking. I could smell his sweat. That isn't normal. It's not a normal thing. I didn't feel sorry for him though. I still don't. I don't care. My job's everything to me. How he felt, when they pulled me away...is how I feel every day, when they walk out of his office.

COUNSELLOR

I am going to have to make a referral to the authorities, you know that don't you?

Only Joking

Posh, rich singleton Will is in group therapy.

WILL

How long have I been coming here? Five years? Five long years of me moaning, that's what you're thinking! Forbes magazine, dozens of young hotties queuing up to be my wife. I can understand how it was difficult for people to empathise. But all I wanted was to find that special connection with that special person. I'll be honest, in the beginning I thought I could treat 'group therapy' as a sort of dating service. People I hadn't met before. Fresh blood so to speak…wonderful. But now that Caroline and I are together. I suppose I've achieved what I set out to. That is allowed, isn't it? It's not a breach of your rules?

COUNSELLOR

So, you and Caroline are together? I didn't know.

CAROLINE

I was going to tell you.

WILL

She is literally the best thing that's ever happened to me!

Caroline, next to him, grins at him, reaches over, and takes his hand. Will grins back.

WILL

Look at me. My skin is growing back. I've stopped the scratching and the tics. I think I'm happy. I think it's time for me to move on. I've come to tell you this is my last session. It's not hers, obviously. She's a fucking nut job.

Murmurs of disapproval.

Aw, come on. It's only a fucking joke! What is this? A fucking concentration camp? A man's entitled to joke occasionally, isn't he? Oh, come on.

Good Grief

Stella is struggling to come to terms with losing her husband. She is at a bereavement counselling session.

STELLA

I was wondering whether there were any mindfulness techniques that I could learn so that I can take my mind off something that's happened recently. My husband died three months ago in a car crash. And I'm thinking about him all the time.

COUNSELLOR

That's so brave of you, Stella. Thank you for sharing that with us.

STELLA

It's quite exhausting. But I've done some reading and a technique is that you can count beads? This is a bracelet he bought me actually. And then there's another where you flick a band on your wrist. I don't want to sound stupid but I think I'm doing it wrong? Because I'm not feeling any better. So, I just wondered whether you could help me do it right?

COUNSELLOR

Mindfulness is a useful tool, but I'm not sure it's useful in every situation.

STELLA

Oh. So, what is there to help me then? You see, my family are getting increasingly fed up with me because I can't stop crying. And I know what they want. They're wanting me to move on. I do understand that. I can't. Every morning when I wake up I expect him to be lying next to me stroking my hair. But he isn't. And every morning when I wake up it's like fresh news. Reminding me. I've tried to discuss this with my family. They are really supportive, they really, really are supportive. But I sense there's increasing tension in the family. Well…well I've had my turn now. Thanks very much for listening.

COUNSELLOR

Well done, Stella.

Anger Management

Carl, a boxer with anger issues, is in a therapy session.

THERAPIST

So how have you been since last week?

CARL

Alright.

THERAPIST

Did you have time to reflect upon what we were talking about in the last session?

CARL

Nah.

THERAPIST

Okay. Well, we were talking about your boxing, weren't we? Because you used to be an athlete. So, tell me about boxing and your anger.

CARL

You don't get angry in the ring. It clouds your judgement.

THERAPIST

I think this week it's important to think about your triggers.

CARL

I think I know what my triggers are…

THERAPIST

Okay. Great! What are they?

CARL

Boasters. Narcissists. Flash Harrys. Basically, anyone who thinks they're better than me.

THERAPIST

Could you develop on that for me?

CARL

Well, they're not better than me, are they? On technical form alone, I'm UK top ten easy. And these arseholes don't come anywhere close.

THERAPIST

So how does it work? They start bragging in the ring and you start seeing red?

CARL

Me and my trainer used to watch their interviews and videos for strengths and weaknesses. Trouble is when I'm in the ring with them all I can hear is them talking about which supermodel they've fucked. Which supercar wants them for a fucking commercial. Who gets to climb Mount fucking Everest. Who gets to spend celebrity golf weekends with Mike Tyson and Tiger Woods.

THERAPIST

Calm down, Carl.

Carl throws his water at the wall.

CARL

Why isn't it me?! Why is it never fucking me?! Why? Why isn't it me?! Why is it never me?

Long pause as he calms down.

Why is it never me? I'm sorry. I…I've got a lot going on. We'll pick this up next week.

Spinning Plates

Jade is in a group therapy session with some colleagues, trying to calm her anger, when all her feelings about her colleagues suddenly start pouring out.

JADE

Anger management is a complete joke! This session is a complete joke! Every time I come here, I listen to your pathetic stories, your mundane complaints, your one-sided fucking views and it just makes me angrier. How's that supposed to help me? And this one here.

She gestures at a colleague.

She can't even bear to look at me! She joined the company the same time as me and I don't think I've ever heard her speak...

GROUP MEMBER

I speak...

JADE

Oh! Now she's vocal. That's to show me up. Anything any of you do is always to make me look bad. I'm forced into coming here...to this bullshit *(in a condescending voice)* 'occupational therapy' because Matthew hasn't got the balls to fire me.

GROUP LEADER

Do you want him to fire you, Jade? Because if this is how you speak to people in the office, I'm surprised he doesn't...

JADE

Are you calling me a bully now? Bully, bully, bully... Because I'm not. I'm just angry.

GROUP LEADER

Why are you angry?

JADE

I'm angry because it feels like nobody's listening...well, apart from Matthew. He's always stood up for me. You don't know what I've been through. My sister's selling her body. My brother's dealing again. I'm the one who tries to hold us together, because my mum sure as hell ain't. This isn't work's problem. I get it, but at the same time you don't know what's going on in a person's life when you judge them for not turning up to Friday drinks, or for getting in late some mornings. You don't know how many plates I'm spinning underneath my desk, so cut the attitude and be kind. That's all I ask.

The Affair

Ray is in couples therapy with his wife. She has just confessed to having an affair.

RAY

I thought you said he was helping you with....

WIFE

Ray, I'm so sorry.

RAY

But you were at work? I can't get my head round this. So Lee picked you up from the office an hour before your shift ended...and then...where did you do it? In our bed? Did you do it in our bed?

Ray gets upset.

WIFE

Ray...

RAY

I feel sick. You must be laughing at me for being so stupid.

WIFE

No.

RAY

You've made a fool of me. All the things that are special to me, he's seen them. He's been in my house, living my life. How can I live my own life in the same way ever again? I can't.

Doing my Bit

Former teacher, Hazel, is suffering from PTSD after having witnessed the suicide of one of her pupils.

HAZEL

Two hours beforehand and you wouldn't have known anything was wrong. I mean, he had a difficult home life, we were all aware of that...but nobody had expected him to jump off the roof. It was 4.30 in the afternoon. I was going home a bit earlier that day, so I was the first one to see him up there...and the last one to see him alive. There wasn't even enough time to shout to him. He was on the ground before I realised what was happening.

COUNSELLOR

You can't blame yourself....

HAZEL

I don't blame myself! I absolutely don't. I didn't sign up to be a social worker, so please explain to me why social work takes up most of my day. I do everything I can to help these kids and it's not my job. I blame their stupid, selfish parents, who can't be bothered to look up from their phones long enough in the right direction to see their children are in trouble. And I blame the government, for cutting services to the parents who do care, but can't cope. I'm doing my bit. Why can't everyone else do theirs?

Work

Binary Code

Rowena has her male colleague bound and gagged on the pool table opposite her. She has a cue in her hands.

ROWENA

Do you know what binary code is, Trev? Because I could always draw an aide-memoire on your scrotal sack if you want?

Victim groans.

ROWENA

You might like it. It's just that now you're my manager, you're going to need to know what all those pretty little figures are…that I put in the computer box. Ten times. Ten bloody times I get passed over for promotion all for some bloke that's been in the company five minutes but does have the required genitals. I wonder what would have happened if I'd've had surgery down there. But even then, I'd have to get it out or wave it around for anyone to know...what? What?!

Rowena takes the gag out of his mouth. The victim splutters.

VICTIM

I'm not the manager, Ro...you're the manager. We all got an email.

ROWENA

Fuck off Trev, you never sent me an email. I'm not that stupid.

VICTIM

You got an email.

ROWENA

Checks her e-mail.

Actually Trev, I just need to...I just need to nip out. Okay? Oh Jesus...what have I done?

She leaves the room.

VICTIM

Ro, I won't tell anyone you drugged me if we can still do that thing Ro...Ro?

Bitch Boss

A boss is ruthless and doesn't let anything stand in the way of getting the job done, not even her worker's chemo session.

BOSS

So, do you want the good news or the bad news first? I'm going to need you to work late again.

WORKER

But thing is today…

BOSS

Sorry, but the client's website goes live in twenty-four hours.

WORKER

Right, but this…

BOSS

I know, I know you've got your chemo session tonight, that's why you can't work late. Don't worry about it. I called them up. And changed it. I pushed it back to Thursday. But that's where the good news comes in. I will be providing private healthcare as an employee perk from now on. Well, actually it's not definite. But you will be getting a free consultation as part of the trial next week, that I can guarantee.

WORKER

You changed my appointment?

BOSS

Oh, it's still with your usual doctor, with the NHS.

WORKER

Do you even know the first thing about…?

BOSS

Watch your tone. You cannot possibly finish the graphics properly in hospital. Too many distractions. Do you understand what I'm saying to you? You do want this job, don't you?

Boss gets a phone call.

Where are you? You naughty boy! I'm coming naughty boy.

Just the Job

Tasmin is a nervous but excited new starter in the marketing team. She's with another newbie having her induction.

HR LEAD

So that's us in a nutshell. Do either of you have any questions?

TASMIN

Yeah, this looks great, really excited to get started, but I've noticed there aren't any computers around, do you need me to bring my own in?

OTHER NEWBIE

Oh, I don't know how to do computer…

HR LEAD

Don't worry. You're not going to need a computer here!

The other newbie is relieved.

TASMIN

Oh…

Suddenly smiling.

Oh! I get it. This is an ideas space, where we just brainstorm and pitch strategy…

She looks around.

Yeah, this could work.

Pretends she's addressing an audience while the other two watch her astonished.

Uh, we need a whiteboard and some pens.

HR LEAD

Uh, we don't have a whiteboard and some pens…but you can have this bucket *(to other newbie)* and you can have this spray.

TASMIN

Props, nice…yeah, I could pitch this…its light, it's bright, it gets the job done…bucket. Why not?

HR LEAD

Just mop the floor.

TASMIN

She looks at the newbie who has already started cleaning.

Sorry, I thought this was a marketing assistant job.

HR LEAD

No…it's a cleaning job.

OTHER NEWBIE

You didn't do so bad.

Desperate Measures

Straight-talking nanny, Anna, is trying to persuade a police officer that her employer has her work permit, so he needs to come back later to check her papers.

ANNA

My employer put my papers in the safe. She's not here right now. It's just me and the baby. Could you come back later? Please.

POLICE OFFICER

Do you know why I don't believe you?

ANNA

I'm telling the truth!

POLICE OFFICER

Because you were never issued a work permit.

ANNA

Maybe you didn't see me here.

POLICE OFFICER

What?

Anna starts to unbutton her top.

Stop...stop.

ANNA

Please. Please I can't go back. Please. You don't know what it's like. I really can't.

POLICE OFFICER

Stop.

ANNA

Please. I will do... anything.

POLICE OFFICER

No.

ANNA

Please.

Anna makes an attempt to seduce the police officer. As it looks like he is about to give in, his colleague arrives.

SECOND OFFICER

The baby's fine.

Both officers leave, leaving Anna alone as the baby cries. Realising what she almost did, Anna begins to cry.

Under Threat of Pineapple

Will believes he is the reincarnation of a medieval warrior. He is in the staff kitchen with his colleagues. His amusement turns to anger when he realises his colleagues don't believe him.

WOMAN

I feel a bit underdressed now.

WILL

No, it's a lovely…sailor's hat. I'll be wearing all of this in a couple of weeks at the big show. You should come along! It'll be fun. You can bring your daggers along. I'll be in charge of the right flank. Just don't get decapitated.

WOMAN

Yeah, that sounds amazing…it's a date.

WILL

I'll send you an email. Cheers! May the quaffing commence!

CO-WORKER 1

I can't believe they've only given us thirty minutes for lunch. I'm knackered. We need to get back in half an hour.

WILL

Half an hour? It takes me an hour to get this stuff off!

CO-WORKER 2

Well, I can take the afternoon show if you're feeling tired.

WILL

Only William DeBohan, first Earl of Northamptonshire, has the authority here to take us into battle.

CO-WORKER 2

Yeah yeah, easy Will.

WILL

Do you want to challenge me? I was placed in charge of the first division by his majesty King Edward himself. I'll fight you.

CO-WORKER 2

Right, stop being annoying now. You're being a prick.

WILL

Do you mock me?

Will holds a sword out in a threatening way.

CO-WORKER 2

Put it away.

CO-WORKER 1

I'll report you to Keith.

WILL

You can tell this Keith that I'll fight him as well.

CO-WORKER 1

Oh god, he's definitely gone method again! (*To co-worker 2*) We need to distract him with a pineapple. They didn't come to Britain till the 1600s. Here you are.

Co-worker 2 picks up a pineapple and gets closer to Will with it.

WILL

Er…don't touch me with it. I'm allergic. It'll bring me out in a rash!

The co-workers laugh at Will and move closer, trying to touch him with the pineapple.

CO-WORKER 2

Stanislavsky would be proud of this one here.

WILL

Seriously guys! Fuck off with the pineapple. I haven't got any antihistamine on me!

Sister's Blessing

Laura's having a moan to her sister. She's pissed off with work and the pandemic.

LAURA

I went four whole days without seeing a real person. All the meetings are online and they're relentless. Also, why do they think it's okay to be so bloody rude, when it's a video call? I can't stand it. I've got no social life and work is just shit.

SISTER

You're like a stuck record. Take the theatre job.

LAURA

What?! Chelle, don't joke.

SISTER

I'm not joking.

LAURA

When I told you about it, you went on and on about how it had taken me nine years to get to Band 6 and what the hell was I thinking?

SISTER

I've had second thoughts. It's only money. I really think this might be good for you.

LAURA

This is really stupid, but you don't know how much that means to me. I know it's weird that I'm going to take a huge pay cut and that I'm going to work my way up from the bottom again, but I want to try it. It's something I've always wanted to...well, you know...and I don't know...thank you. I just needed to hear you say it, have your blessing, before I went for it. You hate theatre!

SISTER

Mum would be proud of you whatever...and I am too

Driving School Dream

Rob hates his job but is unwilling to change it. He looks for excuses to avoid taking responsibility for his own life and happiness. He is in an office, looking at his computer and talking to a colleague.

ROB

I'd have more freedom if I was in prison. Every day this fucking screen. I don't care where the cables go anymore. Heap them up like spaghetti. Why not? Except then I'll have Simmo on my case again. Fucking Simmo. He's ten years younger than me, did you know that?

COLLEAGUE

Yep.

ROB

And he only comes in twice a week. The rest of the time he's working on his golf swing.

COLLEAGUE

You hate golf!

ROB

That's not the point. I should have left twenty years ago, set up the driving school like I planned, instead of giving the money to my son to do it. He didn't do it. Blew it all on bad decisions and status symbols. That mistake sealed my fate. I couldn't afford to get out then. I was trapped.

COLLEAGUE

You can afford it now.

ROB

It's pointless now. I'm too old.

COLLEAGUE

Rubbish. Do it. Do it now. Simmo's a moron. He'll struggle without you. That would show him. Quit and follow your dream. Don't waste any more time. I was looking for driving lessons for my kids and there are no good schools around here.

ROB

Really? I could do it you know. I saw the perfect car for it the other day…Peugeot 108, but really high spec…

COLLEAGUE

Do it!

ROB

Alright. I will.

Rob leaps up.

Midlife Crunch

Exhausted but endlessly patient Roz is trying to sort out the laundry, at the same time as taking repetitive phone calls from her mother with dementia, and all before going to work. Her phone rings:

ROZ

Hi mum, I left it on the table for you. No one's going to take it. Okay. Yeah, that's fine. Yes. I'm coming to see you tomorrow. Yes, look…look mum, I've got to go. Alright? I've got to be back in twenty minutes. Alright. Bye mum.

Roz hangs up, resumes sorting out the laundry. Her phone rings again.

Yes, I've left it on the table for you. No. The carer did not take it. Okay fine. Tomorrow. Yes. You will see me tomorrow. Alright? Bye Mum.

Roz hangs up and finishes the laundry. She finds the pair of tights she needed. Her phone rings again.

Mum, I've left it on the table for you. No one is going to find it and I will be there tomorrow…

Roz pulls on her tights and makes a ladder. She swears. Her phone rings. Her husband appears and hands over a bag of doughnuts and a coffee.

HUSBAND

Hey hey hey. Eat one of them. I'll take this.

She goes to pick up her phone and her husband stops her. He picks it up with one hand. With the other hand, he hands Roz a doughnut and mouths 'I'll give you a lift to work'.

ROZ

Thank you!

HUSBAND

Ay up Doris, it's Mark. No, no one's taken your money. Roz left it on the table for you. Don't worry, it's locked. I checked. No, no one's taken your money. It'll be fine. We'll see you tomorrow, alright? Alright.

Roz hugs him and kisses his cheek.

Alright. We need to get you to work, don't we?

ROZ

Thank you.

Double Agent

Michael is a highly professional double agent who has started to believe the hype about himself and become complacent. He is being debriefed by two of his superiors who have discovered his side hustle.

MICHAEL

(*Laughing.*) It's like you're still operating in 2006. Why don't you give me a call when you've worked out how to use RSA encryption, because until then, nothing you do is safe. It's embarrassing. You're leaking intel like a fucking colander.

BOSS 1

RSA didn't help you, did it? We know you're working for the Chinese Government.

MICHAEL

What? That's not true.

BOSS 2

(*Mimics him.*)

That's not true. Is that your best defence?

MICHAEL

Ningbo Campus, Shanghai. 4th August. The WeMessage leak. That's what you're talking about, isn't it? Check your whistle-blowers, man. I think you'll find I was in St Petersburg having a massage. The one with the twigs and shit. They're brutal, those Russians. When they give you a happy ending, it's painful.

BOSS 1

We know where you were.

MICHAEL

Then you'll know I wasn't online. I found out about the breach two hours after it happened.

BOSS 2

We're not stupid, Mr. Vernon. We have a trace that shows us exactly what you did.

Michael quickly gets up to leave.

Curriculum Vitae

Ed has a job interview that is going exceptionally well, too well. This is because the interviewer has the wrong CV for him.

INTERVIEWER

Your CV is seriously impressive!

ED

Thanks. I got my MSE last week, so I added that, even though the graduation isn't until July.

INTERVIEWER

Right. And all this experience! You did a stint at NASA, the Pentagon, you were in the war room there! Wow! And tell me, what was it like working with Elon?

ED

Er, is that a metal? I guess I was just fitting the car parts, so, uh...?

The interviewer holds up the CV so Ed can see the words Elon Musk. He realises it's not his CV. It's not even his passport photo on it. The name on the CV is Simon Netinyahu.

INTERVIEWER

You're so funny, Simon! Elon Musk though. He's changing the world. I truly believe he'll put a man on Mars...

ED

Uh, yeah. Me too. He's a great guy.

INTERVIEWER

If it was up to me, based on this CV, we'd shake hands now and go out to lunch. A done deal. But I'd better ask you a bit about yourself.

ED

Right. Yeah. Well, NASA was amazing. I mean I got to work on the Space Station, you know, testing things...and at the Pentagon, I was testing things in the situation room. High pressure, but I guess I'm good at working to deadlines so...and as for Elon Musk, his next generation of Tesla is insane! I tested it you know!

INTERVIEWER

Fantastic! That'll do. Let's go and have lunch!

On the Run

Dai is a naive HGV driver, who can't resist money or the temptation of an adventure. He is whispering urgently to his friend in the corner. He has been caught up in a trafficking ring but is desperate not to reveal the real reason for his sudden urge to leave the country.

DAI

Forget all this crap and come to Morocco with me. I've got money. We can hire a 4x4 and drive up into the Atlas Mountains. Make a change from the HGVs! You ever been there? It's stunning. We can camp out. Eat wild fruit. Go windsurfing. Whatever you want. We'll be safe there.

FRIEND

Safe from what?

DAI

Safe from...all this boring shit. Same old faces. No hope. No prospects.

FRIEND

Please tell me this isn't to do with Simon.

DAI

What?

FRIEND

Fuck! It is, isn't it. He's the one behind all those migrants coming over...

DAI

I didn't know what he was doing, I swear! You've got to believe me. I know it's really stupid, but when he said don't open the doors, I didn't. I thought it was drugs, not people. One of them was dead on arrival. A father. His kids were just sitting there looking at me...

FRIEND

Fucking hell. What did you do?

DAI

I ran, but it's not going to take long for them to trace it back to me. I've got to get out of the country. Are you coming or not?

Waking the Lion

Confident Helena's shock turns to delight and then nervousness when a younger co-worker (on whom she has a crush) unexpectedly turns flirty during their pool tournament. She brings over the drinks.

HELENA

Has everyone else gone home?

CO-WORKER

Yeah, but they've got the big presentation tomorrow. They need their beauty sleep. We've done our bit, so we can just relax. (*Points to the glass.*) Is that mine?

HELENA

Strongbow and a bag of dry roasted. That's what you said, isn't it?

CO-WORKER

Thank you. Hey, did you see the peanut display? Each time someone buys a bag of peanuts, a bit more of the naked girl is revealed! How is that allowed in this day and age?

HELENA

You won't remember this, you weren't even born in fact, but in the 80s every pub had a Page Three girl selling peanuts. Now I'm guessing they're claiming it's tongue-in-cheek. Ironic. Some shit like that. It's just Soho moustache types trying to bring porn back to the mainstream. The patriarchy never really goes away, it just grows different facial hair.

CO-WORKER

Woah. I woke the lion!

HELEN

I was approached to do glamour modelling once!

CO-WORKER

I'm not surprised. You're very pretty.

HELENA

Right, your next drink is a coke. You've obviously had a few too many.

The co-worker stops playing pool and looks into her eyes.

CO-WORKER

I'm serious. You're hot! Especially when you're angry.

HELENA

There's a whole feminist part of my brain that's telling me to be offended right now.

CO-WORKER

Well can you ask it if it would like to come back to mine?

HELENA

I've asked. And it would.

They kiss/embrace/touch hands. Hurriedly they put down their cues and leave.

Serious Complaints

Make-up artist Kevin is doing a last check on the performer's make up as he also wraps up his impromptu counselling session.

KEVIN

Right. Don't think of this as make-up. Think of it as warpaint! He can see you from the bar, but don't turn away from him tonight. It's your last show so let him see you in your full glory. Trust me, it's going to hurt him more to let him know what he's missing. You're basically torturing him.

PERFORMER

He came into my dressing room last night when I was showering. Nobody saw him. I only realised after...

Kevin stops applying make-up and stares at the performer in horror.

KEVIN

No! No! No! It's too much. They can't ignore it any longer. I don't care how cheap he's letting them have this place...I'm going to speak to Dan. He'll listen to me!

PERFORMER

No, please don't.

Kevin aggressively pulls on his jacket, just as the stage manager appears.

STAGE MANAGER

Five minutes! Is she ready?

KEVIN

It's not happening! The show's off until you confront that pervert out there and tell him to stop creeping around the dressing rooms! And pestering them, giving them unwanted gifts. He's a bloody weirdo. He's sick! And what's worse…is not listening to the cast when they complain, especially about something as serious as this. If I was handing out bags of bodily fluid, I'd be fired on the spot…

Kevin clocks the stage manager's horrified expression.

You didn't know?

Kevin turns to the performer.

You didn't tell him?

Coat Rage

When the make-up artist finally arrives, the performer, Layla, recognises her. She realises that this was the woman who stole her coat the previous night at the night club.

MAKE-UP ARTIST

Alright. Sophie's ill, so she phoned me.

The make-up artist gets out her make-up and starts laying it out in front of her. Layla stays silent until she starts applying the make-up.

LAYLA

Really? We're doing that, are we?

The make-up artist ignores her and continues applying the make-up.

LAYLA

I know you recognise me. You took my coat. Last night. From the Bodega? This is unbelievable. STEEEEEVE! STEVE! COME IN HERE!

MAKE-UP ARTIST

What? I don't know what you're talking about.

LAYLA

Yes you bloody do! You've got some cheek you have. Where's my coat? Give me my coat back! Steve'll be here in a minute. Wait till he hears about this! STEEEEEEEEVE!

Maternity Leave

A make-up artist is applying make-up to the performer when the director, Phil, walks in.

PHIL

Hi. Where is she?

PERFORMER

Er...in hospital, probably.

PHIL

Excuse me. What?

PERFORMER

Her waters had broken.

PHIL

Sorry. What waters?

PERFORMER

She's...having a baby?

PHIL

What the actual fuck? I didn't know that. Did you know that? How am I the only one who doesn't know that?

MAKE-UP ARTIST

I don't know.

PHIL

How long does having a baby take?

PERFORMER

Quite a while.

PHIL

Great! She's off the show then isn't she! She's off the fucking show! Fuck me. I can't deal with this right now! Do me a fucking favour. Ring her and tell her she's off the fucking show. Secret baby. Unbelievable! (*Calls through the door*) Get Lila from casting here NOW.

Phil storms off leaving the performer and make-up artist sharing dismayed looks.

Un-be-fuck-in-lievable!

Hope, Crushed

Extrovert former administrator Leah is in make-up getting ready for her big break into acting, chatting happily to the make-up artist.

LEAH

I've done all the basics. Crowd scene at a Bollywood flash mob, had a pint in the Queen Vic while Phil Mitchell clears the bar, even Crimewatch! But this is it now. Eight lines. My character's dominating the first scene of the whole series. I couldn't believe it. My agent couldn't believe it. Vicky McClure got her big break with this director…and well, look at her now!

MAKE-UP ARTIST

Good for you. I'm pleased for you.

The production manager walks into the room.

PRODUCTION MANAGER

Leah? Who's Leah?

LEAH

Here!

PRODUCTION MANAGER

Leah! Hi! I'm Michael. Am I right in thinking you're with the studio admin. department?

LEAH

Yes, but I'm booked onto this production in an acting role.

Another woman enters the room, dressed in the same outfit as Leah.

PRODUCTION MANAGER

Yeah, you were, but we've had to switch things around. Helen called. On any other day, this would be fine, but they need you in payroll to help with the self-assessment forms. Some of the girls have missed the deadline and...

LEAH

No, no, no.

PRODUCTION MANAGER

I'm sorry.

Leah crumples into a heap, all hope crushed.

A Ratings Winner

Frustrated soap star, Kerry, is in make-up, moaning to the make-up artist about her storyline.

KERRY

So I'm his cousin and his girlfriend, but it's not technically incest? Can you explain to me, how that's not incest?

MAKE-UP ARTIST

Nope!

KERRY

Obviously, I don't mind doing an incest storyline. That's a ratings winner. Nobody's going to complain about being given that part, but I don't see how my character can be dating my cousin and nobody even mentions it. It's not a thing. In my book that would definitely be a thing!

Suddenly music can be heard outside the dressing room.

Ooooh!

Kerry spins around, just in time to see her boyfriend sweep into the dressing room, in a suit, with a rose between his teeth.

Babe! What are you doing here?

The boyfriend gets down on one knee and offers her a ring in a box.

Kerry gets up and squeals.

Yes! Yes! Yessssssss!

Family and Relationships

Scuppered

Laura is fun, decisive and headstrong. She and her friend grin at each other and clink glasses.

LAURA

Mojitos on the Hudson! This time next week!

FRIEND

I can't wait!

LAURA

Do you know how long I've wanted to go on this cruise?

FRIEND

And now we're finally going!

LAURA

And we're doing it in style! We've got an all-inclusive drinks package!

FRIEND

So excited!

LAURA

We're going to see the world!

Laura shrieks and does a little excited dance. Her friend laughs at her, also happy. Laura then sees her brother heading towards her.

LAURA

Oh hey...Malcolm? What are you doing here?

MALCOLM

You weren't answering your phone. It's Mum. She's had a stroke. I've got to get you to the hospital.

LAURA

What...Now?

MALCOLM

Yes Laura. Now! It's really bad. She's still unconscious and I've got to be in Syria tomorrow. She's going to need you.

FRIEND

But what about our trip?

LAURA

I mean, how long's recovery going to take?

MALCOLM

What?

LAURA

How long will it take her to recover? I'm going on my cruise on Monday.

MALCOLM

You're going to have to cancel it…

LAURA

Cancel it? Why me? I won't get my money back. Here's a thing, why don't you cancel Syria?

MALCOLM

Are you seriously saying that you drinking cocktails for a month is more important than my aid work?

LAURA

Aid work! Oh, fuck off Malcolm. Is that what bonking lonely war widows is called?

MALCOLM

Look. I live there. I work there. You live here. You work here. Now you tell me what it is you're not following about that? Hey? Now are you coming or what?

Laura looks as if she's going to hit her brother, then manages to restrain herself. She turns to her friend.

LAURA

Just put those mojitos on ice. I'll give you a call later…

Leaving

Timid Vanessa must have the confrontation with her partner she's been dreading in order to protect her child.

VANESSA

We need to talk.

PARTNER

Well, get on with it then. I've got another five MOTs to be getting on with. And what are you doing here? Ben's earwigging outside. Couldn't this have waited?

VANESSA

No, no, it couldn't. I'm sorry. But I'm going to my mum's, I'm taking Dylan with me. And I've come here cos I don't want you coming after us.

PARTNER

Where's Dylan now? Is he already at your mum's? He is, isn't he?

He approaches Vanessa and slams hands on table.

This is not happening. This is NOT happening! You go. I'll get Dylan. He's staying with me.

VANESSA

No Rob…no. He's scared of being in the house. He sees the bruises. He hears everything. He's scared of you. And I've told Ben everything and he's on my side. And he's got your keys. So, you can't follow us.

PARTNER

Look, Nessa, you can't do this…look Nessa, I can't cope without you. Nessa, don't do this. I'm sorry! Look, I'm sorry! Just you can't…

VANESSA

I'm going.

PARTNER

You can't leave me!

Vanessa leaves him and the partner turns away.

Right to Choose

Karl's girlfriend has just found out she's pregnant.

GIRLFRIEND

I've got something to tell you…I'm pregnant.

KARL

Oh my god. I'm going to be a dad? Oh my god, I'm going to be a dad! This is amazing.

Hugs girlfriend, who looks conflicted.

I mean, I'll have to tell Mum. When can we even tell people? How long have you even known?

GIRLFRIEND

I took the test this morning. I'm not keeping it, Karl.

KARL

What? Oh no, no, no. Don't do that. Megan, don't do that. Listen, this is going to make things better. This is just what we needed.

GIRLFRIEND

I'm sorry.

KARL

No! Megan, I get a say in this too. This is my child. I'm not going to let you murder my child. It's against God. My son...my daughter...he...she has a right to live. They're already living.

GIRLFRIEND

I'm not ready...

KARL

I'm not going to let you do this.

GIRLFRIEND

I've made my decision.

Mature Attraction

Raquel is trying to make sense of the catfishing Tinder date sitting opposite her. He used an older photo to lure her in and she's not sure how to take the fact the young man wants a sexual relationship with her.

YOUNG MAN

So, what's your poison?

RAQUEL

I'll have a glass of white if you've got one?

YOUNG MAN

Yep.

RAQUEL

You look very young!

YOUNG MAN

Yeah…I kind of used a different photo.

RAQUEL

What? Different photo?

YOUNG MAN

Yeah…

RAQUEL

Catfishing it's called. Isn't it? My daughter told me about that. She is worried to death that I'm going to be suckered into being some pensioner's lover/carer. But you couldn't have submitted a photo of you when you were older. So…

YOUNG MAN

Uhm, I just really like you. When we were chatting, didn't it feel like we had a special connection?

RAQUEL

Well, yeah. And you're absolutely right. If I'd known just how attractive you are I probably wouldn't have answered your first message. And…we're here now…and you look very mature. And you know…there's a lot of advantages to an older woman. Do we even have to go out?

YOUNG MAN

Do I have a choice?

RAQUEL

Nope.

Starting Again

Clare's date is going badly. She's under-confident and realises she should have stood her ground and insisted on meeting him on neutral ground, rather than agreeing to have this friend of a friend cook her a meal in his kitchen.

CLARE

Hey, it's fine. Don't worry about it. I'm not even that keen on coconut.

GUY

If I'd known that I wouldn't have chosen a recipe with coconut.

CLARE

I'm not sure this was a good idea...

GUY

I asked Matt for a full list of everything you don't like. Cocunut wasn't on it. There was lobster...scallops...

CLARE

Interrupting him

Wait, you asked Matt for a list? He didn't say anything to me...although I think we once had a conversation about my allergy to shellfish...

GUY

... oysters.... mussels...

CLARE

Did he name all the different types of shellfish? That's... thorough! So, do you know Matt from school?

GUY

He was my teacher.

CLARE

Ah.

GUY

Uhm, I think I'm a bit autistic. You don't mind, do you?

CLARE

No, no, no! I don't mind at all. In fact, I was quite surprised when Matt set us up on this date, because you know you and I have known of each other for such a long time, and I hadn't even realised that you'd noticed me...sorry, forget that. Start again. I like you, Greg. I like you a lot. So why don't we just stop messing around and take this to the bedroom?

Ultimatum

Phil is a confident and accomplished keynote speaker. He's very relaxed about the affair he's been having with Mariam because he's been taking his perfect life for granted. The two of them are on a break at a conference.

PHIL

Mariam… Mariam please, please, don't send it. Please don't send the message. You're happily married to Raoul. I've always respected that. 'No strings.' That's what you said.

MARIAM

Is that what I said?

PHIL

Outside the Four Seasons in New York, we were standing on the pavement after the first conference and it had just started to snow.

MARIAM

Yeah. I remember.

PHIL

So, what are you playing at then? It's a sex thing, that's what you always said.

MARIAM

Yeah.

PHIL

That's how I've always taken it. Nothing's changed. I don't appreciate being threatened. I thought we had an understanding?

MARIA

Raoul doesn't exist. I made him up. I've been in love with you all along.

PHIL

Oh SHIT! Don't cry. Please don't cry. This is a lot for me to take in... I've loved it. I've loved every minute of it. The things we've done have been wonderful, wonderful. Don't you see? My hands are tied. I've got Amanda and the kids, the business, the house. You're the most beautiful woman in the room, every time. I just wish I'd met you first.

MARIAM

Really?

PHIL

Of course! Of course!

MARIAM

Then tell Amanda! And then we can be together. Just tell her.

Hope

Zoe's husband is trying to persuade her that no more can be done to help her father. The hospital has asked her to consider switching off the ventilator.

ZOE

I don't understand all these numbers. A ten per cent chance sounds better to me than none at all. I mean if we switch off the ventilator, then he's got zero per cent chance. Zero per cent chance to live.

ZOE'S HUSBAND

A ninety per cent chance of failure. It's obvious. Isn't it?

ZOE

But he's my dad. And he's still alive. He's still talking and he knows what he wants. He's told me, he wants the operation. Even though it's a high risk, he wants it. I've got to honour his wishes. Maybe it's just, maybe it's a moment of clarity. And he's you know…he knows he understands what I'm telling him. He wants the operation.

ZOE'S HUSBAND

If that's what you want.

ZOE

I just can't imagine him not…not being here and he's always been here. How can he not be here? He's my dad. He's not ready to go. I love him.

ZOE'S HUSBAND

Whatever happens, we'll be alright. Won't we?

Name Your Price

Justin is in the kitchen with his date Fiona drinking wine.

JUSTIN

I can't wait for you to try this wine. Go on, give it a taste. It's good. You want a stock tip? Forget everything that you've heard about start-ups and get in there early. Lay down a seed investment until you've made the right choice and here you are…it paid for this house. Even if you don't like me for my jokes, like me for my gold AmEx! I'm kidding, obviously. I made my ex-wife a very wealthy woman, you know. Thank you, GitHub.

FIONA

Right.

JUSTIN

Before you, I'd been on so many disastrous first dates, I could have written a sitcom about it. A well-funded one anyway! I don't know if it's because we've been going out since…July, or because you're just so incredibly enticing, but we seem to have this deep connection and I think we should kick things up a notch. What do you say?

FIONA

Justin, I don't...

JUSTIN

Hey! Whoa, whoa. Hey easy, easy. Hey. Wow. Calm down, well the look on your face! Argh! I wasn't going to propose. I know you don't feel the same way and that's okay. But I'm sorry, I've made up my mind. Fiona Willis. Whatever it costs to be together. I'll pay it. Name your price.

FIONA

I've just remembered I left my hair straighteners on. So, I'm...I'm going to have to go.

Fiona leaves Justin's flat.

JUSTIN

Oh well.

The Ex

Laura is having a great time with a friend making dinner, when her ex Jayden walks in and upsets the moment.

FRIEND

Tell me all about it.

LAURA

Oh my god. The concert was amazing.

FRIEND

So gutted I missed it!

LAURA

Hayley gets me up on stage. 20,000 people all staring at me and I don't even have to sing. All I have to do is say my name, into the microphone. So I get the microphone and I yell… Jackie!

FRIEND

Who's Jackie?

LAURA

My aunty!

FRIEND

Your aunty?

They both burst out laughing.

FRIEND

I'm just so proud of how far you've come. And I just want to say cheers to the future.

LAURA

Thank you.

Jayden walks into the room.

LAURA

What are you doing? You can't just walk in here. I…I've had the locks changed.

JAYDEN

You don't know me at all, do you? After fifteen years. I'm disappointed. Anyway, I just came for my work shoes. I left them in the wardrobe.

LAURA

No, they're not Jayden. I threw them out with everything else.

JAYDEN

What?! Are you stupid? They're Italian leather! They were £800!

FRIEND

Chill out Jayden.

JAYDEN

Who are you telling to calm down, you skanky little bitch? I've not forgotten what you did.

LAURA

I think you should leave.

JAYDEN

Shut up. I'm not going anywhere. I still pay the bills for this place.

LAURA

I want you to go.

FRIEND

She wants you to leave.

JAYDEN

I've warned you. Speak again and I'll rip your neck off your shoulders.

Laura holds up a knife to Jayden's throat. Crying as she threatens him.

LAURA

And now I'm warning you. I want you to go. Get out! Get. Out.

Jayden leaves and Laura takes a while to compose herself.

I'm sorry about that. Shall we have some food? Uh, excuse my fingers…

Priorities

Tamsin's little girl has just been diagnosed with leukaemia. She is struggling to explain to her girlfriend exactly what that means and what's going to happen.

GIRLFRIEND

How can you say that? I love her like my own!

TAMSIN

I know you do. And I know she's not your daughter and you do love her like she's your own. This isn't the reason why I'm doing this.

GIRLFRIEND

I'll stop. Okay? Please.

TAMSIN

You know when Tia was diagnosed with leukaemia, it was like well, my whole world fell apart. But it really helped me to put things into perspective. That I need to dedicate all my time to her now. And I just can't give you the time you need and deserve. But you've still got time to start your own family.

GIRLFRIEND

I don't.

TAMSIN

Please don't make this any harder than what it already is.

GIRLFRIEND

You know I want a baby. More than anything. I can't even look at you right now.

Girlfriend leaves.

Man to Man

Mark is a father full of regrets. He sees that his son is as headstrong and stubborn as he once was.

MARK

Look. You go ahead! Divorce her. If that's what you want. But you make sure you've got a good legal team or else she'll block your access to the kids. That's what your Mum did to me.

SON

Sophie wouldn't do that. I know she wouldn't.

MARK

That's what I said. Fifteen years down the line and here we finally are. Mind you, I didn't think she'd really go through with it. God, I was so arrogant. She won't leave you. She needs the money…I should have groveled. That's what I should have done. Apologised at the very least. I spent the night with another woman. Why did I think that was okay? It wasn't okay.

SON

Look Dad, it's different, what I did…it's different.

Silence.

MARK

You've been married to this woman for five years. Do you still love her? It's a simple question. She supported you through your rugby injury. She's raising your kids. Do you love her?

Son nods.

Then for god's sake man. Tell her.

SON

I will.

MARK

Do.

Last Will and Testament

At the table, gobby Carla is accusing her sister of forcing their father to change his will.

CARLA

Mags, he had late-stage dementia, there's no way he knew what he was doing when he changed his will! You haven't seen him in five years.

MAGS

Here we go...

CARLA

Well, it's true isn't it! You weren't speaking to him, you couldn't even call him. Who's been doing everything? Muggins. I am a mug. I was even wiping his arse, before he got the place in the home. And it was disgusting. You know how he ate. Liver and onions. Tripe and potatoes. What was it about offal? Right to the end. As much as he could keep down in that dicky stomach of his anyway. But at least I loved him. And he signed over everything to you...I didn't get a penny.

MAGS

There's nothing I can do about it. But did you ever stop to consider, Miss Goody Two Shoes, that maybe it was something you did? You didn't, did you?

CARLA

Don't say that. I did everything for him. Everything! Could I have upset him...? Oh god...

A Proposal

Reece is looking down at his girlfriend, on bended knee in front of him. She is proposing.

GIRLFRIEND

Reece?

REECE

Oh sorry...I mean, I wasn't expecting you to do that. Argh! Okay...I mean not okay...

GIRLFRIEND

So it's a no?

REECE

Um...I don't know. It's not a no... just give me a minute to think about it. How long have we been going out? Three years...Three and a half years...that's a good amount of time, a long time...and I love you, Cath, I do, I really do...you're amazing. And I like your family too! I want to spend the rest of my life with you...I think, it's just...

GIRLFRIEND

It's Emily, isn't it? Be honest...

The girlfriend stands up.

REECE

Alright. This feels like it might be a trap, but I'm going to be honest. She was my first love and she broke my heart. I'll probably always wonder what it would have been like to marry her...oh no. Your face. You didn't want to hear that, did you?

GIRLFRIEND

Not at this moment, no.

REECE

Does this mean it's over? I was happy five minutes ago. What just happened?!

Wait for Me

Sam is a cheeky charmer whose life has taken a serious turn recently. His wants to leave his wife and loveless marriage for his girlfriend but he knows his family will react badly.

SAM

My wife's going to be back any minute. She's only at the shop. I haven't had the chance to tell her I'm leaving yet, but I will, I promise. It's just hard. She's going to be upset and I need to handle it sensitively or she won't let me see the kids.

GIRLFRIEND

She knows. I've just seen her and she ignored me. I said hello. We both reached for the same choc ice. She definitely knew I was there...

SAM

Don't worry about her. It's her mother you need to worry about. And mine. They're going to kill me, and then you...oh no. Don't look like that. It'll be fine. We'll be fine. It's just going to...you need to give me a bit of time to sort this all out.

GIRLFRIEND

You still want this…to move in with me, don't you? You're not just making excuses?

SAM

Babe no! Me and her were never compatible. The stars got it wrong. Fucking stars! You're the one I should have met twenty years ago. Now we just need to make up for lost time…wait for me, okay?

Moral Relativity

Hilary has found an envelope containing £100,000 in her daughter's bedroom. When confronted, her daughter told Hilary that she has the cash because a friend who sold her house gave it to her for safekeeping.

HILARY

It's in an envelope in her bedside drawer. You don't need to touch it or do anything with it. Margie's going to pick it up in a fortnight. I just wanted you to know.

HUSBAND

But I don't understand. It's a hundred grand and you think she's stolen it. Shouldn't you make her give it back?

HILARY

I don't know she's stolen it! I didn't say that! All I said was it was strange she left the bank so suddenly. I thought she liked that job. I don't know what's going on with it and I don't want to know.

HUSBAND

If she needed financial help, she could have come to us.

HILARY

I know that. And I've always said that to her. But don't you see, just supposing this money isn't exactly legit…she can't just hand it back without consequences. She could go to jail. I don't want to send my daughter to jail. And what about baby Joshie? Do you think we'll see him at all if Andy's in charge?

HUSBAND

I'm really not happy about this.

HILARY

Phil, please! This is my daughter! Please! Just leave it be and she says it'll be gone soon. I don't want this either, but what can I do??

HUSBAND

Tell the police. If you don't, I might…

HILARY

No! Don't you dare! Phil. No!

Hilary starts to cry.

I Love the Flow

Happy-go-lucky commitment-phobe Rohan has come to the flat to pick up his girlfriend, only to find she's not there and he's confronted with her mother.

ROHAN

Hi, is Lucy here?

SHEILA

Hi, you must be Rohan. I'm her mum. Sheila. Come in.

ROHAN

Oh, it's okay. I'll just wait here till she's ready

SHEILA

I won't bite! Please, come in. She's told us a lot about you.

ROHAN

Okay. Do you think she'll be long?

Rohan shuffles in with his hands in his pockets. There are some DVDs on the kitchen counter.

ROHAN

Bruce Lee? Has Lucy got another fella?

SHEILA

Oh, those are mine dear. I got them from the charity shop. I love the flow of Wing Chun. And the storylines of course.

ROHAN

No way. *Fist of Fury* is a classic. They don't come better than that! Lucy has a cool mum!

Sheila takes some baklava out the oven.

SHEILA

It's hot but would you like a piece?

ROHAN

Yes please! That is my absolute favourite.

Rohan eats a piece and very obviously enjoys it.

SHEILA

You're such a delight, Rohan. Will you be coming to tea at our house on Sunday? I asked Lucy to invite you. We can put on the *One-Armed Swordsman* afterwards, while they wash up! Jimmy Wang chopping everyone in his path. What's not to like!

ROHAN

Thank you. I'd love to, Sheila.

SHEILA

I might have to grab hold of you in the scary bits…

ROHAN

Er…right…

Sheila runs her hand up his arm to feel his muscles.

SHEILA

Impressive! Do you work out?

Lucy walks into the room.

LUCY

Hi, shall we get going?

ROHAN

Hi! Yeah!

While Rohan hurriedly heads for the door, Lucy turns round and gives her mum a secret thumbs up. Sheila winks back. When they've left, Sheila smells the baklava, makes a face, and chucks it in the bin. Rohan re-enters and grabs Lucy's bag which she's forgotten. Sheila turns to look at him. He winks at her.

ROHAN

I'm looking forward to Sunday!

Running Around

Warren and his girlfriend have just come in from a run.

WARREN

Did you enjoy that?

GIRLFRIEND

It was hardcore! My glutes are protesting! What made you pick that route?

WARREN

Hang on, let me show you the GPS.

Warren hands his girlfriend his phone.

GIRLFRIEND

Oh, that looks weird. Like it's spelling out a word. Oh! Does it say "marry me"?

WARREN

Look in your phone pouch…

The girlfriend takes her phone pouch off her arm and looks inside. She pulls out a ring. Warren sinks to his knees.

WARREN

Will you marry me, Jess? I never thought I'd feel this way about anyone, and this is a huge cliché, but you complete me. We've been together for three years and I've never been happier. I want us to be forever. What do you say? Jess? Jess? You're making me nervous.

GIRLFRIEND

I slept with Mark.

WARREN

My friend Mark?

GIRLFRIEND

I'm sorry!

WARREN

I can't believe it.

GIRLFRIEND

I don't think we can get married. I don't think we can even stay together. Mark and I...

WARREN

Mark. Fucking Mark. No. No. This isn't how it ends. I'm not allowing it. Listen to me Jess. I'll kill him if I have to, but you're not doing this to me. DO YOU HEAR ME?

Activism

Extinction Rebellion member Florence has a massive crush on the activist sitting opposite her and the feeling is mutual. However, Florence is also angry that he has been shouting at commuters during their last protest.

FLORENCE

God you're sexy in that top. It's a bit distracting!

ACTIVIST

That's good, because from the face on you, I thought I was going to get a bollocking.

FLORENCE

You still are. It's just…sorry. Lost my train of thought there.
Talks to herself.
Come on Flo! Come on Queen! Pull yourself together.
Lightly slaps herself.
Alright. Mark, listen. I know you're passionate…
Mark moves closer.

ACTIVIST

I am very passionate!

FLORENCE

Don't! What you did today is not okay! Those commuters are not the enemy. They're cross because we were blocking the road. With good reason I might add. When we reverse climate change, they'll be chucking gratitude all over us. But my point is, you cannot key a car in the name of the cause. In any name. It's just vandalism.

ACTIVIST

Oh, we didn't just key it. We torched it! We want people to know we're serious, don't we?

FLORENCE

You did what?!! You torched that car? That's arson. That's a really bad crime. Mark! I can't believe you did that. What did the guy say? The one who's car it was?

ACTIVIST

I dunno. I didn't see him again.

FLORENCE

Mark, he wasn't in the car, was he? Tell me he wasn't in the car!

Acknowledgements

I'd like to say a huge thank you to our writer-in-residence Sara Bodinar, with whom I am blessed to have collaborated on this book and a variety of ongoing creative projects. And many thanks to our editor, Fiona Robertson, who has been a driving force behind this book, as well as our previous publication *Monologues for Showreels*. Fiona, we couldn't have done it without you. I'm also really grateful to our willing and diligent proof-readers, Denise Morton and Tom Russell, and to Jemima Osborne, for all her careful work on the scenes and the QR codes.

Finally, we would like to give thanks to all the actors whose scenes are featured in this book. We are so proud to celebrate their creative achievements. If you are a film-maker, producer or casting director, we recommend you hire them now before they get booked up!

About Screen School

Screen School courses explore the skills required for film and television acting. Through practical exercises and daily teaching sessions, attendees gain the screen-acting knowledge needed to work in front of the camera. During the course, actors are provided with a script, rehearse their scenes and receive focused direction. The course culminates in the filming of the scenes. The high-quality showreel footage is then edited and provided as showreel material to share with agents and casting directors. Our courses are suitable for both complete beginners and more experienced performers.

For more, please visit screenschool.uk

About the Actors Workshop

The Actors Workshop Nottingham & Online provides an opportunity for adults to explore and develop the necessary skills for careers in film, television and radio. Through acting workshops, drama classes, private one-to-one tuition, and focused screen acting courses, we strive to both nurture new talent and enhance the skills of experienced actors. Numerous students have benefitted from casting opportunities in film, television, voiceover and corporate videos. Our alumni now appear on screens and stages across the world.

If you would like to know more, please visit: actorsworkshoponline.com

Printed in Great Britain
by Amazon